Peachy + Paolo Abellera

PAOLO

ABELLERA

WONDERFUL WORLD OF KNOWLEDGE

YEAR BOOK 1986

Wonderful World of Knowledge

YEAR BOOK 1986

GROLIER ENTERPRISES, INC.
Danbury, Connecticut

ROBERT B. CLARKE   *Publisher*

FERN L. MAMBERG   *Executive Editor*

MICHÈLE A. MCLEAN   *Art Director*

MARGARET M. FINA   *Production Managers*
ALAN PHELPS

ISBN 0-7172-8184-1
The Library of Congress Catalog Card Number: 78-66149

Text on pages 36-39, 62-65, 92-95, 110-113,
and all Disney character illustrations
Copyright © 1986, Walt Disney Productions

COPYRIGHT © 1986 BY GROLIER
INCORPORATED
DANBURY, CONN.

Copyright © in Canada 1986 BY GROLIER LIMITED

PRINTED IN THE UNITED STATES OF AMERICA

Grolier Enterprises Inc. offers a varied
selection of both adult and children's book
racks. For details on ordering, please write
to: Grolier Enterprises Inc., Sherman Turnpike,
Danbury, CT 06816, Attn: Premium Department.

CONTENTS

1985 AT A GLANCE

JANUARY 3. Edwin Meese III was named U.S. Attorney General, to succeed William French Smith. James A. Baker III was named U.S. Secretary of the Treasury, to succeed Donald T. Regan.

JANUARY 10. Donald P. Hodel was named U.S. Secretary of the Interior, to succeed William P. Clark. John S. Herrington was named U.S. Secretary of Energy, to succeed Hodel. William J. Bennett was named U.S. Secretary of Education, to succeed Terrel H. Bell.

JANUARY 20. Ronald W. Reagan and George H. Bush were sworn in for their second terms as, respectively, president and vice-president of the United States. At 73, Reagan was the oldest president ever to be sworn in.

JANUARY 27. The U.S. space shuttle *Discovery* completed a three-day mission. It was the first time a shuttle flight was devoted exclusively to secret military objectives. It was reported that the five-member crew had deployed an intelligence-gathering satellite that could "eavesdrop" on Soviet telecommunications.

FEBRUARY 8. Vernon A. Walters was named U.S. Ambassador to the United Nations, to succeed Jeane J. Kirkpatrick.

FEBRUARY 24. It was announced that the Nature Conservancy, a U.S. environmental group, had agreed to buy seventeen acres of desert near Lucerne Valley, California, in order to protect the world's oldest known plant. The plant, a creosote bush, is about 11,700 years old—more than twice as old as the previous record

holder, a 5,000-year-old bristlecone pine. Creosote bushes are found throughout the southwestern United States and Mexico. They get their name from the creosote-like smell that is given off when their leaves are crushed.

MARCH 10. Soviet leader Konstantin U. Chernenko died at the age of 73, thirteen months after he had assumed power. (On March 11, Mikhail S. Gorbachev was chosen to succeed Chernenko as general secretary of the Communist Party's Central Committee. This is the most important position in the Soviet Union. At 54, Gorbachev became the youngest person to lead the U.S.S.R. since Joseph Stalin came to power in 1924, at age 45.)

MARCH 15. Raymond J. Donovan resigned as U.S. Secretary of Labor after a New York state judge ordered him to stand trial on larceny and fraud charges. Donovan was the first U.S. cabinet member ever to be indicted while in office. (On March 20, William E. Brock III was named to succeed Donovan.)

APRIL 19. The space shuttle *Discovery* completed a seven-day mission. The seven-member crew included Senator Jake Garn of Utah, the first member of Congress to take part in a space mission.

MAY 1. Declaring a national emergency, U.S. President Ronald Reagan ordered an embargo on trade with Nicaragua and banned Nicaraguan aircraft and ships from the United States. Reagan said that Nicaraguan policies and actions were a threat to the security of the United States.

MAY 15. It was announced that scientists had found the skeleton of the earliest dinosaur yet discovered. The bones, found in the Painted Desert in Arizona, were estimated to be 225,000,000 years old. They belonged to a plant-eating animal that had a long neck and tail and was about the size of a small ostrich.

JUNE 12. Spain and Portugal signed a treaty admitting them to the European Economic Community (the Common Market), as of January 1, 1986. (The treaty was ratified, as required, by the parliaments of Spain, Portugal, and the organization's ten member nations—Belgium, Britain, Denmark, France, Greece, Ireland, Italy, Luxembourg, the Netherlands, and West Germany.)

JUNE 14. A Trans World Airlines plane with 153 people on board was hijacked by Lebanese Shi'ite Muslims shortly after takeoff from Athens, Greece. Over the next two days, the plane was forced to fly back and forth between Beirut, Lebanon, and Algiers, Algeria. It finally landed in Beirut. During that time, one passenger was killed and more than 100 others were freed by the terrorists. By June 19, 40 hostages, all American men, were still being held.

Except for the three crew members, who were held on the plane, the men were hidden in various locations in Beirut. The hostages were finally released on June 30, under an agreement mediated by Syria.

JULY 13. U.S. Vice-President George Bush served as acting president for eight hours while Ronald Reagan underwent surgery for removal of a cancerous growth in his large intestine. (Reagan made a quick recovery, and he was released from the hospital on July 20.)

JULY 20. Salvagers discovered off the coast of Key West, Florida, a Spanish galleon (ship) that had sunk in 1622. The galleon, the *Neustra Señora de Atocha,* contained silver, gold, and other treasures worth $400,000,000. ■ Following months of unrest in black townships, the government of South Africa declared a state of emergency in 36 cities and towns. Hundreds of people, most of them black, were detained. The unrest stemmed largely from opposition to apartheid, the government's policy of racial segregation and white minority rule that discriminates against blacks.

AUGUST 12. A Japan Air Lines plane carrying 524 people crashed into a mountain range in central Japan. Only four people survived the crash. It was history's worst air disaster involving a single plane.

SEPTEMBER 2. A team of American and French researchers reported that they had found the wreckage of the *Titanic,* the luxury liner that sank on its maiden voyage in 1912, after colliding with an iceberg. More than 1,500 passengers and crew lost their lives; some 700 escaped in lifeboats. The wreckage was found about 500 miles (800 kilometers) southeast of Newfoundland. The researchers used an unmanned, remote-controlled submarine, the *Argo,* to locate the wreck. The *Argo* was connected by a long cable to a research ship on the ocean's surface. It was equipped with searchlights that illuminated the ocean floor, and its cameras took thousands of photographs of the sunken ship. The photographs showed that the *Titanic* was still largely intact and upright.

SEPTEMBER 19–20. Two earthquakes caused massive destruction in southwestern Mexico. The greatest damage and loss of life occurred in the capital, Mexico City. More than 5,500 people were killed, and tens of thousands were left homeless.

OCTOBER 7. Four Palestinian terrorists hijacked an Italian cruise ship, the *Achille Lauro,* off the coast of Egypt. The hijackers demanded that Israel free 50 Palestinian prisoners in exchange for the release of the passengers and crew. On October 9, the ship sailed into Port Said, Egypt, and the hijackers surrendered after being promised safe passage out of Egypt. It then became known that the terrorists had killed one of the ship's passengers, an American man in a wheelchair. The following day, an Egyptian plane carrying the hijackers to Tunisia was intercepted by U.S. planes and forced to land in Italy. There, the terrorists were taken into custody.

NOVEMBER 6. The space shuttle *Challenger* ended a seven-day scientific mission directed by West Germany. It was the first time a foreign country had managed a shuttle flight. Aboard the shuttle were eight astronauts—the largest shuttle crew ever.

NOVEMBER 7. Otis R. Bowen was named U.S. Secretary of Health and Human Services, to succeed Margaret M. Heckler.

NOVEMBER 13. A volcano in northern Colombia erupted, creating mud avalanches that buried one town and devastated others. An estimated 25,000 people were killed in the disaster.

NOVEMBER 21. U.S. President Ronald Reagan and Soviet leader Mikhail Gorbachev ended a two-day summit meeting in Geneva, Switzerland. It was the first meeting between U.S. and Soviet leaders in six years. Reagan and Gorbachev discussed arms control, regional conflicts, human rights, and other topics in sessions that were said to be frank and direct. The two leaders had differing views on these issues, but they announced agreements on cultural exchanges, airline safety, and new consulates. The talks were seen as a promising sign for better U.S.-Soviet relations.

NOVEMBER 23. An Egyptian jetliner en route from Greece to Egypt was hijacked by Palestinian terrorists and forced to fly to Malta. The terrorists shot several people, two of whom died. (On November 24, Egyptian troops stormed the plane, and 57 passengers, crew members, and hijackers died in the rescue attempt.)

DECEMBER 27. Palestinian terrorists fired at crowds of travelers in airports in Rome, Italy, and Vienna, Austria. Nineteen people, including five Americans and four terrorists, were killed.

A ROBOT UNDER YOUR ROOF?

The alarm rings, waking you up. Moments later a robot enters your bedroom.

"Good morning," it says. "The school bus will be here in one hour. Remember to take the history report that's due today. You have soccer practice after school, so take your gear. And your parents want you home by 5:30 because Aunt Mary is coming for dinner."

You get up, rubbing the sleep from your eyes. As you head toward the bathroom, you say, "Heat some water for cocoa and make two pieces of toast."

The robot moves toward the kitchen to carry out your request.

An imaginary scene? Yes . . . but not for long. The day is coming when robots will be common household objects, ready to carry out all sorts of chores—from vacuuming and washing windows to preparing meals.

MECHANICAL SERVANTS

For thousands of years people have dreamed of building machines that look and act like people. Greek mythology tells of a giant mechanical man (automaton) made of bronze that guarded the island of Crete. In the 1700's, Europeans enjoyed watching doll-like automatons that could write, play the piano, and draw pictures. The actual word "robot" was coined in 1921. At that time, Czech playwright Karel Capek wrote a play called *R.U.R.,* about a man who created artificial humans to work in his factory. Capek took the name from the Czech word *robota,* which means "work."

The early automatons were mechanical devices that operated automatically, and they were designed to perform just one task. Today's robots are also mechanical devices that operate automatically. But they can be programmed to do a variety of tasks—because they have computer "brains."

Modern robots aren't necessarily human-like in appearance—in fact, most robots used in factories look like giant mechanical arms. But many home, or personal, robots tend to look at least a little like people. They have a headlike part that may have two "eyes," which are actually light sensors used to detect and avoid objects in the robot's path. An arm, or arms, may be attached to the sides of the body. There may even be legs, although most home robots move about on wheels. Some robots also have artificial voices, but their vocabularies usually aren't very large.

The home robots currently on the market are fairly limited in what they can do. They are designed primarily to perform simple chores, to be entertainment machines, or to be educational devices that teach how robots work. Averaging 2 to 3 feet (60 to 90 centimeters) in height, these robots are usually operated with a remote-control unit. Some of the current popular home robots are Hero 1, Hero Jr., Hubot, Omnibot, F.R.E.D., Topo, B.O.B., and RB5X.

Most home robots can move around the house, usually on a programmed path. One model, Hubot, moves with the push of a button or a verbal command. This robot has a serving tray and a voice, so it can be put to work as a butler. You can, for instance, teach it the path from your kitchen to a specific chair in your living room. Program in some welcoming phrases. Then load its tray with cookies and milk (this robot has no arms), and station it in the kitchen.

Ask a friend to take a seat in your living room, and tell the robot to bring in some refreshments. The robot will move into the living room and head for the chair where your friend has been seated. "Hello. It's good to see you," says the robot. "Please help yourself to cookies and milk."

This robot is more than a butler. It's an entertainment system, too. It has a built-in TV, radio, tape deck, clock, and video-game system. And with special attachments, it can turn appliances on and off, act as a smoke alarm, and even vacuum a rug.

Hero, the most popular home robot, is a squat character with one arm that can be extended and retracted and that can move left, right, up, and down. Its "hand" is a gripper that can pick up and hold small objects. The robot has electronic sensors that detect light, sound, motion, and obstructions in its path.

Hero is the most popular home robot. It has an extendable arm, a gripper hand, and electronic sensors that detect light, sound, motion, and any objects in its path.

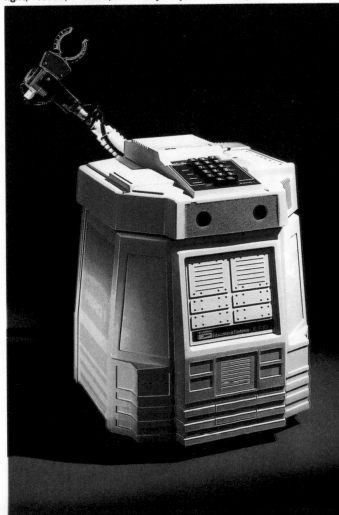

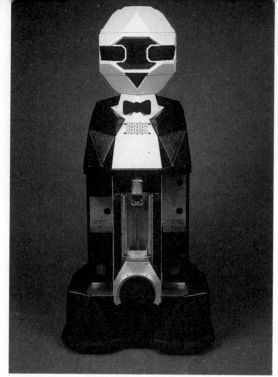

B.O.B. (for *Brains on Board*) talks in a humanlike voice.

Omnibot can wake you up and serve breakfast on a tray.

It can be programmed (through a keypad on its top) to travel over a predetermined course and to carry out certain functions in a pre-determined order. This robot can move from one bedroom to another in the morning, saying "Good morning. Time to rise and shine." It could even be used for walking a dog!

Some robots serve as security guards. Hero Jr., for example, can be programmed to guard in either of two ways: It can be stationary, in front of a window or a door, or it can roam around the home. If its sensors detect any movement, it speaks: "Intruder

alert! Intruder alert! You have five seconds to signal the proper password." If the person gives the correct password, the robot says, "You may pass, friend." But if the correct password isn't given, the robot sets off a loud alarm.

When not acting as a guard, this robot can play games with you, recite poetry, and even sing. "Daisy" and "America the Beautiful" are among the songs in its repertoire.

HIGH-TECH TOYS

Robotic toys have become as popular as the more sophisticated home robots. One young Japanese robot designer has created a whole "zoo" of battery-powered robotic toys, called Movits—most of which have built-in computers. Each is small enough to be held in the palm of your hand, and each has its own unique abilities. One has six legs and an infrared sensor that detects objects in its path. If something is in its way, it stops, turns until it no longer detects the obstruction, and then moves off in a new direction. Another Movit moves along a path that you can create. This may be a line drawn on a piece of paper or a black tape track that you lay down on the floor. The robot uses infrared light to follow the path. Still another

RB5X sings and plays a game called "Spin the Robot."

Movit can be programmed to go right, left, or straight ahead, and to beep or flash its headlight as it travels.

Movits are sold as do-it-yourself kits. Their computers are tiny microchips mounted on printed circuit boards, and they are already assembled. The only tools needed to put together one of these robot toys are a screwdriver and a pair of needle-nose pliers.

Other robotics engineers are designing robotic "pets" that bear at least some resemblance to cats and dogs. One such creature is an electronic stuffed animal with a furry coat that purrs when you pet it . . . and meows when it gets stuck in a corner. You can give it a name, and it will come when you call it.

ROBOTS OF TOMORROW

Just as there are imitation cats and dogs, there are imitation robots. You may have met some of these in shopping malls. They are cute creatures that wander up to people and start talking to them—usually saying such things as, "Have you ever talked to a robot before?" But these creatures aren't true robots because they don't contain computers—they are operated by a nearby human using a remote-control device.

Scientists are working on a variety of technologies to make true robots really useful machines in the home. To be more than just sophisticated toys, home robots must be able to hear and understand human speech. They need a sense of depth, so that they can identify and distinguish among various objects.

This robotic Movit can be held in your hand. The toy has a built-in computer and moves along a path you create.

They need a sense of touch, and hands more like human hands than like grippers. They need to be able to climb stairs and open doors.

How long will it be before people have really useful home robots? Experts disagree. Some believe it could take 100 years; optimists say it will take less than 10 years. One thing is certain: Home robots are a fantasy that will come true—eventually!

JENNY TESAR
Designer, Computer Programs

This robotic "cat" purrs when you pet it and meows when it gets stuck in a corner.

HANIMALS

Do you know that you have an entire zoo . . . right at your finger-tips? With a bit of imagination and some paint, you can find a zebra in the palm of your hand, maybe a goose or a giraffe between your fingers. Use two hands to create a cocky rooster with a brilliant red comb. Or paint on dots to form the spots of a Dalmation dog; your thumb can make his floppy ear. With a quick sleight of hand (and some gray paint), your thumb can become an elephant's trunk.

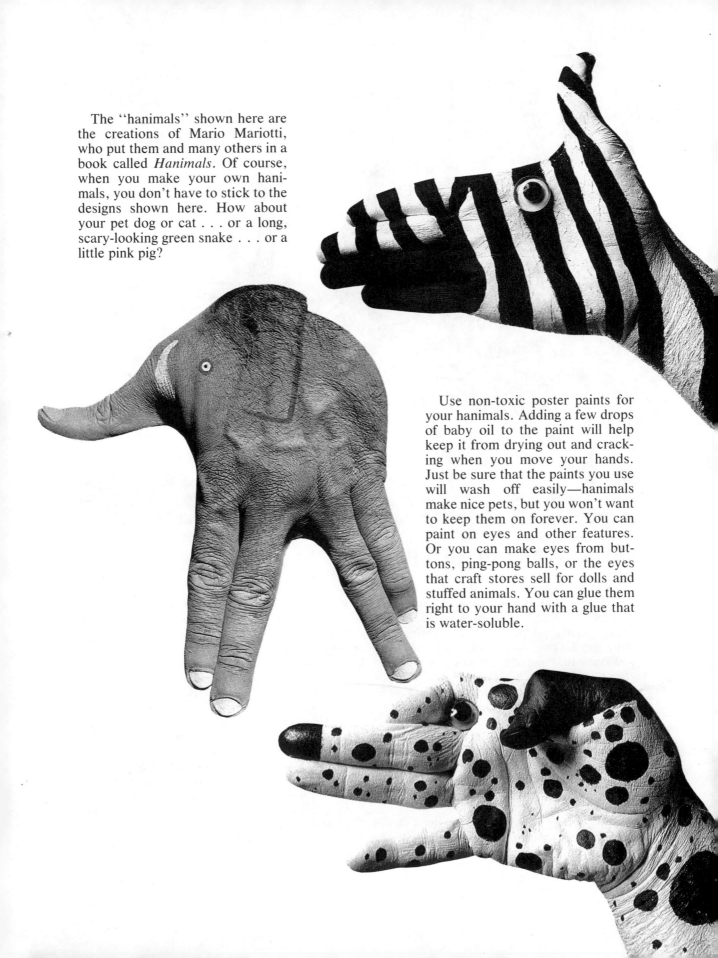

The "hanimals" shown here are the creations of Mario Mariotti, who put them and many others in a book called *Hanimals*. Of course, when you make your own hanimals, you don't have to stick to the designs shown here. How about your pet dog or cat . . . or a long, scary-looking green snake . . . or a little pink pig?

Use non-toxic poster paints for your hanimals. Adding a few drops of baby oil to the paint will help keep it from drying out and cracking when you move your hands. Just be sure that the paints you use will wash off easily—hanimals make nice pets, but you won't want to keep them on forever. You can paint on eyes and other features. Or you can make eyes from buttons, ping-pong balls, or the eyes that craft stores sell for dolls and stuffed animals. You can glue them right to your hand with a glue that is water-soluble.

LET'$ $TART A BU$INE$$!

One thing almost everyone can use more of is money. And that probably includes you. Many young people are discovering that there are lots of ways to earn money. Did you know that one of the best ways is to start your own business?

"But what should I do?" you ask. The answer is simple: provide people with anything they need . . . or want. Some kids bake cookies to sell at local fairs and tag sales. Others raise and sell minnows for bait. Still others sew and sell doll clothes. Here are some guidelines that may help you decide which kind of business would be best for you.

1. What can you do well? A business will be successful only if the product or service you sell is of good quality. Make a list of things you do well. Do you have a green thumb? Start a lawn service, or raise and sell houseplants. Do you speak fluent Spanish? Begin a tutoring service.

2. What do you *like* to do? A business is generally more successful if it revolves around something you enjoy doing. Do you like young children? Then open a child care service. Do you love parties? How about starting a party business—help people plan, set up, and serve at their parties.

3. Do your neighbors need any special service that you might be able to provide? The best way to learn your neighbors' needs is to ask them. For instance, if you have elderly neighbors who don't get out much, ask if they are interested in a grocery shopping service.

4. How will competition affect you? Even if you are providing a desired service or product, your chances of having a successful business will improve if you don't have a lot of competition. Consider, for example, a business involving crafts. Many people make and sell such items as bookmarks, wreaths, placemats, and potholders. Therefore, you should try to create products that are unique —such as personalized T-shirts.

5. How much money do you need to spend to get started? Most businesses require some start-up money. For example, if you are going to create posters for people, you'll need to buy posterboard, construction paper, and paints and brushes. If you are planning to make aprons, you'll have to buy fabric and thread.

Once you've decided what type of business you will have, you must figure out what to charge for your work. One way to do this is to find out what other people are charging for the same service or product and perhaps price your work slightly lower. But remember that if you want to make a profit, you'll have to charge more than what it costs you to make and sell your product.

Sometimes, instead of charging less than your competition, you may want to give your customers something extra. If you have a shoe-shine business, give people a coupon for each pair of shoes you shine. Tell them that you'll give them a free shine when they've collected ten coupons.

Now it's time to let people know about your business. Advertise! Make attractive announcements that can be hung in local stores (be sure to first get the store manager's permission). Distribute flyers in your neighborhood. Make up business cards. (You can write them out on ordinary file cards. Just make sure that each card lists your name and telephone number and clearly indicates what service you provide.)

For some businesses, you may want to make appointments with potential customers. Dress neatly. People are more likely to listen to you—and buy your product—if you look professional. Smile when you introduce yourself, and shake hands. Explain why you're there. If the person isn't interested, keep smiling! Offer him or her one of your cards and say something like, "Please call me if you need this work done in the future."

Many people will say "no" to you. But some will say "yes." And if you do a good job, they will be satisfied customers. They'll call on you again, and they'll recommend you to their friends. That's the way a business—any business—grows and becomes successful.

Let's take a closer look at three areas in which you might start a business.

A PASSION FOR PETS

If you like animals and if there are lots of animal owners in your community, start a business that involves caring for pets. A dog-walking service is a good way to begin.

You don't need any money to start a dog-walking service. You do, however, have to be a very responsible person. Dog owners will probably want you to walk their dogs on a regular schedule. Be sure to stick to the schedule, and always arrive on time.

Agree ahead of time on how long you are to walk the dog. Try to be exact about this time limit. If you bring the dog back early, customers may feel they aren't getting what they're paying for. If you keep the dog out longer, customers may worry that there was

an accident. Remember, too, the value of offering a little extra—an occasional bonus walk or a free brushing.

Sometimes you may not be able to get to your job, perhaps because you are sick or out of town. Try to have someone else available to walk the dog when you can't. It's a good idea to introduce this person to your customers and their pets ahead of time. Go over the route you follow, point out do's and don't's (such as areas where it's illegal to walk dogs), and in general familiarize the person with your routine—and your professional standards.

After a while, you may wish to expand the services you provide. Let customers know that you will groom dogs or take care of them for extended periods of time, such as when owners are on vacation.

You can even sell items related to your service. Pet identification tags, collars, toys, and pet placemats are popular. You can make these yourself or sell them for a friend who makes them. In the latter case, you collect a commission (a percentage of the sale) on every item you sell.

THE CLEAN SCENE

Cleaning may not be your favorite activity, but it can be the basis of a very profitable business because many people *hate* to clean. They dislike cleaning windows and garages and cars and floors and yards. So offer to do it for them!

In planning your business, decide who will provide the cleaning supplies. If you provide them, you can charge more but you'll have to spend money ahead of time. If the customers provide the cleaning supplies, you don't have to spend money and you'll know that you'll be using the products they prefer.

Before offering to clean something, be sure you know how to do it. Cleaning a window is different from cleaning a floor. And cleaning a boat is different from cleaning a car. Your best bet is to learn the job by helping someone who already knows how to do it. If you want to learn to clean cars, for example, find someone who keeps his or her own car shining.

A successful car-washing service can bring in steady money. Try to line up customers by leaving flyers under windshield

22

wipers of cars—especially dirty ones. Once you have your customers, you can keep them by doing a better job than the local car wash. Scrub the tires, clean the mud flaps, and shine the chrome.

Start small and with a service that you can do really well. Then expand. You may want to offer to clean the interior for an additional fee. (You should vacuum the inside, empty ashtrays, dust the dash, and wash the windows.) Then why not add a waxing service to your car-wash business?

COMPUTER SERVICES

Do you own a computer? Do you know how to use it? Can you write programs on it? Many people want to learn how to use computers. And you can earn money simply by teaching them.

If you are successful doing this, you may want to expand your computer-teaching service into a publishing business. This will be easiest to do if you have a disk drive, a printer, and a word-processing program or a program especially designed for creating newspapers. (Bear in mind, however, that this equipment is very expensive.)

Publish a neighborhood paper, with stories about the people who live and work in your area. Include information on local events, such as soccer games, art shows, and public meetings. Sell the newspaper door-to-door. After you have published several issues and people are familiar with the paper, try to get subscriptions. Ask local store owners if they would like to advertise in the paper. Neighbors who are planning tag sales may wish to place an ad. So may friends who offer baby-sitting and other services.

You might also consider buying a mail-list program. Then you can offer mailing services to local businesses and organizations that send out bulk mailings—that is, notices to large numbers of people. Stores, for example, send out sales flyers, and religious organizations send out newsletters. They do such mailings on a regular basis, and the material usually goes to the same people. Each piece of mail must be addressed—a task that you can accomplish with your computer. The organization provides you with the mailing list and you type it into the computer. Then you print out labels and attach them to

the envelopes. When it comes time to provide the labels for the next mailing, just push a button on the computer and it does all the work faster and less expensively than anyone who is writing or typing the labels.

An important part of a mailing service is keeping the mailing lists up to date. This means adding new names, removing names of people who have moved away, and correcting names and addresses that contain errors. If you're working for more than one organization, keep their mailing lists on separate, clearly marked disks. You'll lose a lot of business if you send material to the wrong mailing list.

With hard work and luck, you may soon find that your part-time business has grown too big for you to handle by yourself. Then it's time to look for assistants. You won't have to look far, for there are lots of kids out there looking for ways to earn some extra money!

NATURE'S PHARMACY

Modern medicine fights disease with a battery of drugs—everything from aspirin to antibiotics. In any drugstore or supermarket, you'll see shelf after shelf of pills, syrups, and ointments designed to treat one ailment or another. We rely on these remedies so completely that it's easy to forget how new most of them are.

But for thousands of years, before these sophisticated remedies were developed, people depended on plants to cure their ills. Indeed, the earliest known medical book—a Sumerian stone tablet 4,000 years old—is a list of the medical uses of plants. The ancient Greeks and Romans also used plants to cure disease.

In Europe and America, right through the 1800's, every garden included herbs for medical use. People gathered these herbs and others that they found growing wild in the countryside and hung them from their rafters to dry. Then they used them to make everything from freckle removers to cures for deadly diseases.

Often people believed that plants had almost magical powers. Some of these beliefs sound funny today. Walnuts, for example, were said to cure brain diseases. As modern medicine developed, the old treatments fell out of use, and pots of herbs were replaced with the bathroom medicine cabinet. But scientists have found that many plants do have medicinal uses—in fact, about thirty percent of modern medicines are made from plants.

What follows is a description of some of the uses people found for common plants in days gone by. A word of caution: If you feel sick, don't go and eat a plant. Some plants can be harmful, and if you're ill you should be under a doctor's care.

BASIL

Common, or sweet, basil is an herb that's often used in cooking today. It's a delicious seasoning for tomato dishes. But this herb has a long and fascinating history. In India, it's a sacred herb—it's grown outside Hindu temples and houses, and a basil leaf is placed on the chest of a person who dies, as a passport to heaven.

In the past, people thought that the strong aroma of basil leaves would disinfect the air. A leaf placed on a bee sting or the bite of a venomous insect was said to draw the poison out and soothe the wound. Scorpions were drawn to basil, it was thought, and superstitious folk believed that basil leaves would turn into scorpions if they were left to rot. One writer even claimed that smelling the leaves would cause a scorpion to grow inside a person's head!

CHAMOMILE

A cup of chamomile tea may well have been your great-grandmother's cure for all the little worries and troubles of life. The tea made from the flowers of this daisylike plant has a strong aroma, something like new-mowed hay. It was said to soothe worries, ease pain, relieve nausea and diarrhea, and prevent nightmares.

Oil made from crushed chamomile flowers was mixed into poultices for toothaches and boils or rubbed onto painful joints. The flowers were also used to make a rinse to add highlights to blond hair. And a wash made from chamomile, roses, and willow bark was said to prevent insect bites.

Today chamomile is still used in soaps and shampoos. And you can find chamomile tea in the supermarket—many people still think that it soothes away some ailments.

Basil

Chamomile

Cowslip

Primrose

Dandelion

COWSLIP

The cowslip and its relative the common primrose are native to the English countryside, and these spring-bloomers were in great demand through the 1800's. The flowers were enjoyed as food—mixed in salads and other dishes, candied, pickled, fried, and made into wine. They were believed to cure all sorts of nervous disorders—everything from headaches to palsy.

Juice from the primrose plant was said to cure madness, while cowslip juice put on the skin would remove wrinkles and discolorations. An ointment of primroses and bramble tops was used to treat sores. And tea made from primrose leaves and flowers was touted as a cure for gout, arthritis, and insomnia.

DANDELION

This common plant—the plague of many a lawn—has almost as many old-time medical uses as it does seeds. In Ireland it was thought to prevent passion and swooning. Gypsies used its milky juice to remove warts. Various parts of the plant were used to treat kidney and liver diseases, and it was also thought to help arthritis. Tea brewed from the plant was used as a laxative and as an all-around "blood purifier." The leaves, which in fact are rich in iron, were said to cure anemia.

Like cowslips, dandelions were also popular as food, and many people still enjoy the leaves in salads or as cooked greens. The flowers are used to make dandelion wine,

26

and the roots have been dried, ground, and used to make a tasty coffee substitute.

GARLIC

Garlic is surrounded by superstitions. In ancient Egypt and Rome, people believed that eating it would make you strong. Later, people carried cloves of garlic as a charm against vampires.

The Chinese have used garlic for medical purposes for almost 4,000 years, and in Europe garlic was widely believed to prevent and cure infections. In Germany, garlic was once put in children's stockings or mixed into lard and used as an ointment to ward off whooping cough. Mixed with vinegar and rubbed on the skin, it was supposed to prevent plague. A syrup made of garlic was used for asthma and coughs.

Even today, many people think garlic may help cure diarrhea, rheumatism, and high blood pressure, along with other diseases. Some research has even been done on the use of garlic to treat cancer.

MARIGOLD

These pretty summer flowers brighten many gardens, but in the past they were thought to have great powers. In the 1600's, spice merchants stored dried marigold petals by the barrel for sale throughout the year. And people bought them to cure headaches, toothaches, bee stings, smallpox, measles, and jaundice. Jam made from marigold petals was said to stop heart palpitations, and water distilled from them was used to soothe reddened eyes. A potion made from marigold flowers was also used for fevers, to bring on perspiration.

MINT

The mint family includes many different plants, and most of them have been used medicinally at one time or another. Sprigs of mint were kept around medieval houses to freshen the air, and people drank peppermint tea or ate powdered spearmint leaves to ease stomach cramps and hiccups. Peppermint tea was also used to bring on perspiration in

Peppermint

Garlic

Marigold

fevers. Mint leaves were said to kill fleas, lice, and other pests if they were rubbed right on the skin. Added to a bath or to an ointment, they were believed to soothe aches and pains.

Catmint, or catnip, was used for many of the same purposes. But people also thought that this wild mint (which got its name from the fact that cats love it) had a magical property: Anyone who ate it—no matter how timid—would become fierce and bold.

MUSTARD

When you spread mustard on a hot dog, you probably don't think you're taking medicine. But two varieties of the mustard plant —white mustard and black mustard—were important in the herbal pharmacy.

Mustard plasters (which are mixtures of mustard, flour, and egg white) were used to bring down swelling and draw out splinters. Because the oil contained in the plants is ir-

ritating and stimulates circulation—it can even blister the skin—it was also put into heat-producing liniments for arthritis and rheumatism.

A person might chew a few mustard seeds to ease a toothache, or drink mustard seed tea for rheumatism. Gargling with the tea was said to help a sore throat. And a spoonful of mustard flour mixed in water was used to cure hiccups. Mustard was even thought to restore lost hair and cure snakebite, mushroom poisoning, and leprosy!

NASTURTIUM

This vinelike plant with big, heart-shaped leaves and showy flowers grows wild in South America. In the 1500's, Spanish explorers found it and took it back to Europe with them. There, people quickly found medical uses for the plant. The plant's juice was thought to be an antiseptic, and it was also taken for colds and as a general tonic.

Nasturtium

Mustard plant

Rose

Pansy

But the nasturtium's greatest use was as a cure for scurvy—and in fact, nasturtium leaves contain great quantities of vitamin C. (Unfortunately, people often used the plant's seeds, which contain less of the vitamin, instead of the leaves.) The nasturtium plant was used to treat scurvy right through the 1700's, until lemons and limes were found to be a better cure. Today, many people still enjoy the leaves and flowers in salads.

PANSY

The little wild pansies called Johnny-jump-ups were used to treat bad skin, rheumatism, and heart disease in the past. But there were also many superstitions about them. The name "pansy" comes from the French word *penser,* "to think." In Elizabethan times, people believed that if you went to sleep with pansy juice squeezed on your eyelids, you'd fall madly in love with the first person you saw when you woke up.

ROSE

One of the most magnificent garden flowers, the rose was also one of the most useful medical plants. The ancient Greeks believed that a poultice of rose petals would even cure the bite of a rabid dog. The Romans made at least 32 different medicines from roses. And in medieval Europe, roses were prescribed for almost every illness you can think of.

Red rose petals were preferred for medical uses because they were thought to be stronger than other types. Blended with honey, they were used for sore throats; with vinegar, for headaches. Various other concoctions made from the flowers were said to strengthen the heart, stomach, liver, and memory; to prevent fainting and vomiting; and to cool fevers. But the herbalists who developed these cures never seemed to hit on the real health value of the rose: Rose hips, the fruit of the plant, contain as much as 20 times more vitamin C than oranges.

SHOWERS OF LIGHT

You strain your eyes, searching the dark night sky. Then you hear it: the pop of a distant explosion, followed by a long, whistling *sssst,* and——BOOM! The sky explodes in a shower of a million colored stars, their brilliant glow slowly fading as they drift toward the earth like rain. The fireworks display has begun.

Small wonder that fireworks have been one of the most popular forms of entertainment for centuries—they mix color, light, and sound in a very dramatic way. And in 1985, the Canadian city of Montreal was host to the biggest fireworks show ever staged in North America. It was the International Fireworks Festival, held nightly for three weeks in June. At the show, fireworks companies from all over the world competed to see who could put on the most fabulous display. (These pictures show some of the magnificent fireworks from the festival.)

No one knows for sure just when or how fireworks were invented. The credit usually goes to the Chinese, who were the inventors of gunpowder. (This is the powder that's used to make fireworks.) Arab traders probably brought fireworks from China to Europe. By the 1300's, fireworks displays were becoming popular in Europe as a way of celebrating special events—the coronation of a king, the signing of an important treaty, a religious festival.

Early fireworks displays were usually put on by the military, who were used to handling gunpowder. It was a dangerous business—spectators and fireworks handlers were sometimes killed when the explosions were set off. Later, kings and queens employed firemasters, who were charged with co-ordinating fireworks displays.

Gradually, fireworks developed into an art form. Sometimes, the sky shows were combined with elaborate "set pieces" on the ground. These were specially designed forms —such as a famous building or the portrait of a ruler—outlined with glowing fireworks. One of the most popular pieces was a fire-breathing dragon. To create such pieces, the firemaster employed a whole team of assistants. They would build a frame of willow or whalebone, attach fireworks at strategic points, cover the whole form with papier-mâché, and then set if off, Unfortunately, their creation would last only a moment.

Fireworks displays were often set to music—Handel's *Music for the Royal Fireworks* was written in the mid-1700's for a British fireworks show. Water was another important element. Displays were often staged over lakes and rivers, for safety and so that the brilliance of the fireworks would be reflected in the water.

Fireworks were just as popular in North America as they were in Europe. In the United States, fireworks on the Fourth of July have been a tradition almost since the founding of the nation. At one time, people celebrated the Fourth by setting off fireworks in their own backyards.

In the 1800's, advances in chemistry allowed fireworks masters to create incredibly brilliant colors. (The colors are produced by adding chemical salts to the explosive powder. Strontium salts make red; calcium, orange; copper, blue; and sodium, yellow.) There were also improvements in the original gunpowder formula.

Elaborate set pieces—scenes showing the winning of the Wild West, for example—were the biggest crowd pleasers at this time. In one of the most spectacular shows of the late 1800's, a fireworks maker simulated Niagara Falls by pouring golden showers over the Brooklyn Bridge.

Today home fireworks are banned in most places because they are extremely dangerous. But people continue to enjoy public displays. Skyborne displays are the most popular—rockets that burst into enormous, glowing chrysanthemums or showers of golden fire and smoke, and fountains of fire that shoot up from the ground. And fireworks companies have some new tricks that make their displays more spectacular than ever.

Sometimes fireworks are combined with laser lights that comb the sky. And fireworks are still often set to music. Now, however, they can be set off with a computerized timing device. In this way, the brilliant explosions will be perfectly timed with the concert, whether it be rock or classical.

People still thrill to see the night sky fill with exploding colored stars. Fireworks, it seems, will never go out of style.

YOUNG PHOTOGRAPHERS

Ordinary things are everywhere—a cat, the sun, people's faces. You pass them every day, and you probably never give them a second glance. But the photographs on these pages show that there's more to the ordinary than meets the eye. They were among the winners in the 1985 Scholastic/Kodak Photo Awards Program, which offers scholarships and other awards to junior and senior high school students in the United States and Canada.

The young people who took these pictures have clearly learned that a camera has a unique ability: It can freeze, forever, a moment in time. And when a photograph is well made, it can help us see that moment in a new way. So the next time you go for a walk, take a second look at the ordinary things around you—and take your camera along.

Air Balloon, by Jennifer Slacktish, 14, Jermyn, Pennsylvania

Stoplight, by Paul LaGumina, 18, Burbank, California

Here Comes the Sun,
by John B. Moore, Jr., 17,
Irving, Texas

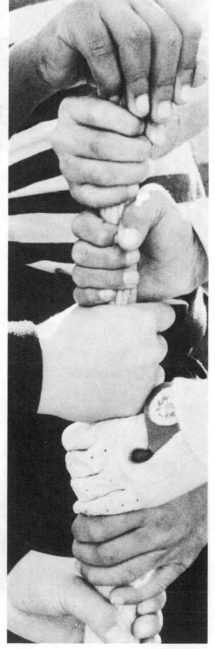

Building Bridges of Friendship,
by Robert A. Alaantara, Jr., 17,
South San Gabriel, California

Eyes of the Past,
by David Martasian, 16,
Sacramento, California

Peek-a-Boo,
by Rhonda Zimmer, 16,
West Frankfort, Illinois

A PUPPY DOG TALE

"Pongo!" called the pretty Dalmation. "Pongo—where are you?"

Her handsome mate lifted his head from the rug in front of the fireplace and blinked to clear the sleep from his eyes. "I'm in here, Perdita," he answered with a wide yawn and a long stretch. "What is it?"

"Pongo!" answered Perdita. "Some of the puppies are missing!"

"Now, Perdy, dear," soothed Pongo, "I'm sure you must be mistaken. Perhaps you miscounted. It would be easy enough to do, with as many as 99."

"I couldn't have," said Perdita. "Nanny was just giving them their dinner, and I counted twice. There are three missing— Rolly and Penny and Lucky. Oh, Pongo, it's that DeVil woman again, I just know it!"

"Now don't panic, dear," said Pongo. "We'll get to the bottom of this. We can check up on Cruella at her London flat. We'll use the Twilight Bark."

Perdita was still uneasy. She remembered when Cruella had stolen her own dear puppies. When she and Pongo had found them, they had also found 84 other spotted pups, all collected by Cruella so she could make herself a fabulous black and white fur coat. After the puppies had been rescued, Roger and Anita, their humans, had kindly taken them in. In fact, Roger's music had become so successful that he had purchased Hell Hall from Cruella and turned it into a "Dalmation plantation."

Perdita was dreadfully afraid that Cruella was up to her old tricks.

Pongo was more worried than he allowed Perdita to see. He went to the big iron gates at the end of the driveway and began to bark. "Woof! Woof! Arf, wuuf, owooo!" he called.

"We'll see if the DeVil woman had anything to do with this," he added to himself.

A hound on Hampstead Heath picked up the message and relayed it to a setter in Soho, who sent the message on to a Scottie in St. John's Wood, which was where Cruella had her townhouse.

The terrier hustled over to Cruella's to investigate. When he looked in a window, he found her in a frenzy of redecorating. She was surrounded by cans of paint and pots of

wallpaper paste, bolts of drapery fabric, and long strips of black and white wallpaper. But no black and white puppies. He dutifully sent the message back to Pongo: "Woof, arf, woof! Woof, rowf! No Dalmation puppies here."

Pongo was relieved to find that Cruella hadn't taken their puppies again. But where could Lucky and Rolly and Penny be? And how was he going to find them?

"Perhaps the Colonel can help," suggested Perdita. So Pongo went to consult the old sheepdog. He found the Colonel dozing on a pile of hay in the barn. Pongo gently nudged his shoulder.

"What? What? What?" said the Colonel, looking around in confusion.

"Colonel," said Pongo, "three of our puppies have disappeared."

The Colonel shook himself from nose to tail. It seemed to shake his brain awake. "Three puppies, you say, old boy? Can't have that. You'd better find 'em."

"We thought you might help us," said Pongo. "You know the terrain so well, after all."

"Quite right," the Colonel agreed. "Let's get Tibs, and we'll put our heads together."

Sergeant Tibs the cat was consulted. Practical as always, he pointed out that they'd have to wait until daylight to make a search. "But as soon as the sun is up," he suggested, "we'll form search parties and comb the grounds."

The Dalmations spent an uneasy night, but when dawn came, they were assembled and listening to the Colonel's orders.

Soon the gardens and woods surrounding the former Hell Hall were covered with busy black and white bodies, noses sniffing the ground and tails wagging as they searched every possible hiding place. One by one, the groups reported back to Sergeant Tibs. No puppies had been found.

The Colonel declared himself stumped. Pongo was out of ideas, and Perdita was beside herself. Then Sergeant Tibs spoke up.

"Did you look inside the Hall, Mrs. Pongo?" he asked.

"Why, not really," she said. "I went to each floor and called, but there was no answer. We don't use the top two floors, you know," she added. "They haven't been remodeled yet."

"It's a strange old place," said the cat. "Cruella's father was something of a practical joker. It's full of doors with no rooms behind them, and stairs that lead nowhere, and cupboards that open into hidden passageways. There's no telling what Lucky and Rolly and Penny may have stumbled upon."

"I never thought of that, Tibs," said the Colonel. "Come on! Back to the Hall!"

A black and white tide streamed back to the "Dalmatian plantation." Again Tibs set up groups to make a thorough search. "No one is to search alone," he cautioned, "and everyone is to check in with me every fifteen minutes."

Carefully the Colonel, Pongo, Perdita, and 96 puppies began to search. They went into every room, opened every door, climbed every stairway. Just as Tibs had said, many of the doors led nowhere, and many of the staircases ended abruptly in walls.

Nevertheless, finally the whole Hall had been searched. Pongo and his group were the only ones who hadn't returned to check in with Sergeant Tibs.

Perdita began to worry even more. "There, there, my dear," said the Colonel, patting her dainty paw clumsily with his big fuzzy one. "Pongo's probably found them. He'll be back any minute."

They waited . . . and waited . . . and waited some more, but no Pongo. Now there were even more Dalmatians missing!

Finally Perdita could stand it no longer. "This is ridiculous," she announced. "I won't sit here and do nothing. Come on, Colonel, Tibs—we must search again."

Up the wide staircase went Perdita and her cohorts, looking carefully for some kind of clue. At the end of the hallway they found a door to another, narrower stairway. Up they climbed, carefully feeling their way along. When Perdita got to the top of the stairs, she bumped into a wall.

puppies, and everyone went tumbling down the stairs.

When they had sorted themselves out and picked themselves up, Perdita found herself looking at Lucky. Behind him were Penny, Rolly, and Pongo.

"Where have you been?" she exclaimed.

"Oh, mother," panted Lucky, "we were exploring . . ."

". . . and we found a secret passage . . ." added Rolly.

". . . and we couldn't get out!" wailed Penny.

"I found the same passage and couldn't get out either," finished Pongo.

"Boy, are we glad you found us!" said Lucky.

"We'll have to go back down," said Perdita. As she turned around, her shoulder brushed against a picture that was hanging on the wall. "What a funny place to hang a picture," she said.

Suddenly there was a creak behind her, and the "wall" began to open!

Sergeant Tibs came forward. "Here, Ma'am—let me," he offered, and he crept forward into the dark passage. "Is anyone there?" he called.

Suddenly Tibs was bowled over by a wriggling black and white mass. He stumbled back into Perdita, the Colonel, and all the

"I guess it's a good thing Lucky got lost," chuckled Pongo.

"How could you say such a thing?" said Perdita. "I've been worried sick."

"Look at it this way, Perdy," Pongo answered. "Without Lucky's luck, we might never have been found."

Perdita looked severely at her mate. Then she looked around at her puppies—all 99 of them. And she smiled.

"Let's go down to dinner," she said. "If Lucky's luck is still holding, Nanny will have made enough for the Colonel and Sergeant Tibs, too."

FLYING HIGH

Look, up in the sky . . . it's a bird, it's a plane, it's . . .

Actually, it *is* a plane. But it's a paper plane—an entry in the Second Great International Paper Airplane Contest. The event was held in Seattle, Washington, in May, 1985 (the first such contest took place in 1967). It was sponsored by the Smithsonian Institution, the Seattle Museum of Flight, and *Science 85* magazine.

THE ENTRIES

More than 4,300 paper airplanes were entered in the contest. They came from all parts of the United States—from Maine to California—and from many foreign countries. Far off places such as Saudi Arabia, Yugoslavia, and Bangladesh were represented. Many entries were sent from Japan, where making paper planes is a popular hobby. One Japanese entrant was the author of books on the subject.

The planes were to be judged in four categories: Time aloft, distance, aerobatics (stunt flying), and aesthetics (beauty). All had to meet basic requirements—they had to be made of paper (a flying beer can was disqualified) and held together with glue or cellophane tape. And the entries quickly proved that there's no limit to imagination where flight is concerned.

Among the simplest entries were paper plates and a wad of paper that arrived with the instruction "hurl very hard." (These were disqualified for not being true planes.) The smallest entry was a glider measuring 1 by 1½ inches (2.5 by 4 centimeters). Among the most elaborate were the entries in the aesthetics category. They included the Superman plane, butterflies, bats, a flying pineapple, and a slime-green papier-mâché lizard that came with instructions to "feed two small rodents daily."

Most of the designers mailed their planes in. The youngest was 3 years old, but more than half the entrants were adults. One contestant sent 28 planes! In each category, the entries were to be judged in two or three

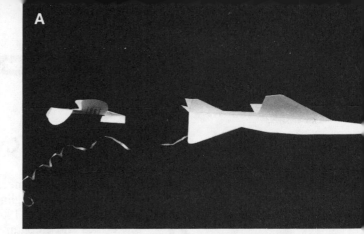

A

separate divisions: professionals (people in the aerospace field), nonprofessionals, and juniors (under 14 years old).

THE WINNERS

After preliminary eliminations, the 250 top planes were brought to Seattle's Kingdome Stadium on May 24, to show whether or not they had the right stuff. Each plane was sent aloft three times by a volunteer and then judged on its performance.

Not all the planes performed as expected —some made detours into the stands, some circled when they should have gone straight, and many made crash landings on the stadium's astroturf. But the winners showed that a piece of paper can be made to do remarkable things. Some were unconventional designs, and their ability to fly fascinated air-and-space designers in the audience.

The aerobatics category provided some of the most exciting flights. The winner in the professional division was a plane that carried a small glider (**A**), by Tatuo Yoshida of Japan. It soared above the field, released the glider, and then circled back to earth.

In the distance category, a classic glider (**B**) made of scrap paper, by Eltin Lucero of Colorado, won in the junior division with a flight of 114 feet, 8 inches (35 meters). The nonprofessional winner, by Robert Meuser of California, flew an amazing 141 feet, 4 inches (43 meters). And the first-place winner in the professional division, by Akio Kobayashi of Japan, made it to 122 feet, 8 inches (37 meters).

A high-wing monoplane (**C**) by Yoshiharu Ishii of Japan stayed aloft 9.8 seconds to win first place in the nonprofessional time aloft category. But longer flights were made by the planes of junior winner Hironori Kurisu (11.28 seconds) and professional winner Tatuo Yoshida (16.06 seconds).

In the aesthetics category, the judges chose a flowing, circular design (**D**) by Masakatsu Omori, also of Japan, as the winner in the professional division.

First-place winners were flown to Seattle, where they demonstrated their paper planes and received awards in a special ceremony. Then the winning planes were put on display at the National Air and Space Museum, in Washington, D.C.

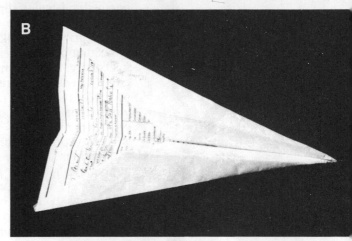

B

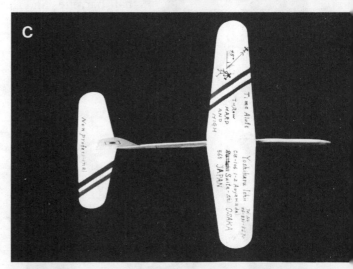

C

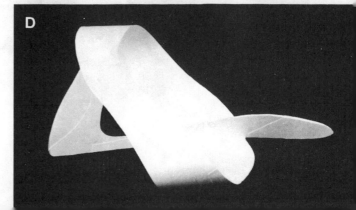

D

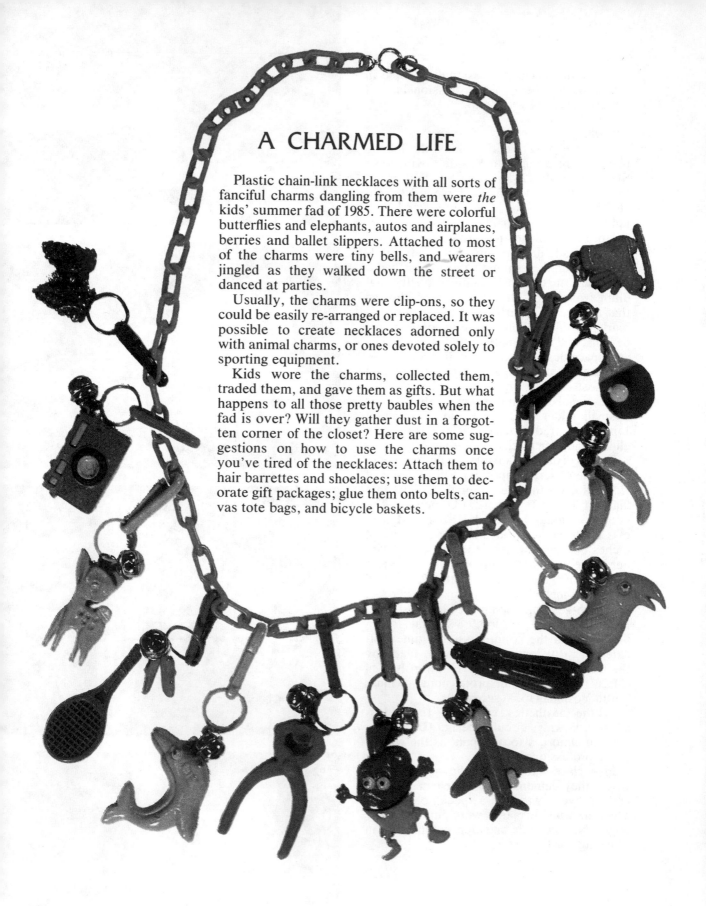

A CHARMED LIFE

Plastic chain-link necklaces with all sorts of fanciful charms dangling from them were *the* kids' summer fad of 1985. There were colorful butterflies and elephants, autos and airplanes, berries and ballet slippers. Attached to most of the charms were tiny bells, and wearers jingled as they walked down the street or danced at parties.

Usually, the charms were clip-ons, so they could be easily re-arranged or replaced. It was possible to create necklaces adorned only with animal charms, or ones devoted solely to sporting equipment.

Kids wore the charms, collected them, traded them, and gave them as gifts. But what happens to all those pretty baubles when the fad is over? Will they gather dust in a forgotten corner of the closet? Here are some suggestions on how to use the charms once you've tired of the necklaces: Attach them to hair barrettes and shoelaces; use them to decorate gift packages; glue them onto belts, canvas tote bags, and bicycle baskets.

THE SECRET MESSAGE

Shirts bearing printed messages have long been popular. But here's a shirt with a message that's meant to be read only by very special people. The message is written in code. Can you decipher it? Use the clues in the box to figure out which letter each symbol represents. Using symbols like these, you and your friends can make up your own code, then use it to write secret messages to one another.

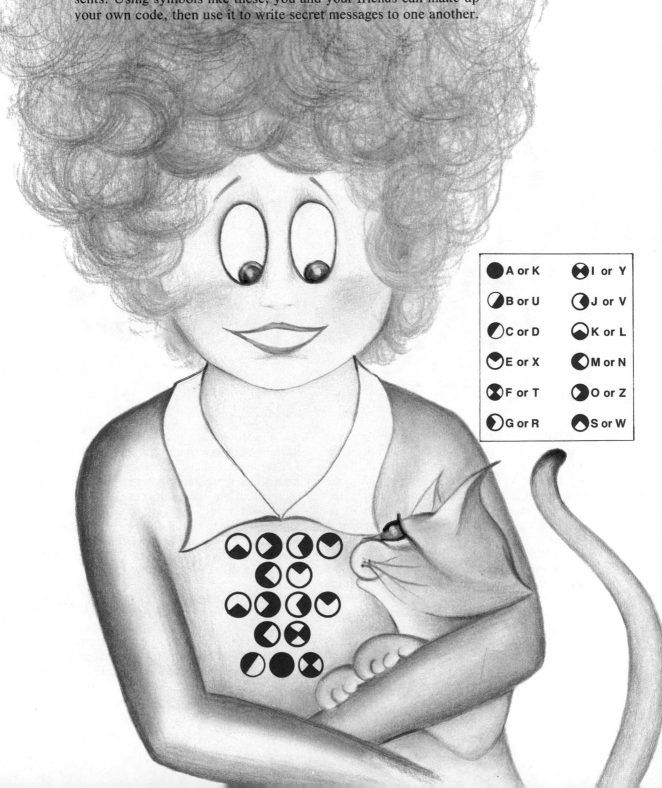

RIDING INTO THE PAST

Back around the turn of the century, life was simpler than it is today. World wars, jet lag, and air pollution were yet to come. People spent cool summer evenings rocking on their front porches. On a Saturday afternoon, if you had a nickel to spend, you might walk down to the corner drugstore for a soda.

Or you might take the trolley to the park at the end of the line for a magical ride on a carousel. Colored lights and mirrors would spin around you, while an organ played a waltz to set your pace and a majestic steed carried you off to an enchanted land. If you were quick—and lucky—you might reach out and grab the brass ring as you whirled past it, and win a second ride for free.

The carousel, or merry-go-round, reached its height of popularity in the early 1900's. Perhaps the makers of carousels at that time knew they were dealing with magic, because their creations were no everyday amusement-park rides. The style, craftsmanship, and attention to detail shown in the wooden horses that pranced around these carousels took them out of the realm of the ordinary and made them truly works of art.

GAMES ON HORSEBACK

The word "carousel" comes from the old Italian word *carosello,* which means "little war." In the Middle Ages, this word was used to describe a game played on horseback, in which riders tossed fragile clay balls filled with perfume to one another. The obvious losers of the game were the horsemen who broke the balls—and were splashed with scent.

The game spread to France, where along with similar games it became part of elaborate horseback pageants called *carrousels*. In one game devised for these pageants, riders had to pierce small rings with their swords. To train for this event, noblemen of the 1600's developed a strange device: They rode on wooden horses that were mounted on beams around a central pole. Servants or live horses pulled the contraption around the circle. And with each revolution, the horsemen tried to spear a brass ring with the tips of their lances.

The device was clearly too much fun to be used only for training. Women and children of the court and even peasants quickly copied the idea, and thus the carousel was born. The rides soon spread to other Euro-

pean countries. But these early rides couldn't carry many people because they were so difficult to propel.

Then, around 1870, a British manufacturer started putting powerful steam engines in his carousels. Now the rides could be made much larger, with several rows of horses, and could carry many more people. They soon became popular features of parks throughout Europe and North America. (British carousels were different from those in other countries in one major way. Most European and American carousels turned counter-clockwise, so that people could grasp the brass ring with their right hands. Those who succeeded might win a free ride. But the British merry-go-rounds traveled clockwise, so that riders would mount their steeds from the proper side—which, as any rider knows, is the left.)

The British carousel makers began another trend: They decorated their wooden

Carousels reached their heyday in America in the early 1900's. And carousel horses were prime examples of the woodcarver's art. This carousel horse has been stripped of its paint, showing the magnificent carving and natural beauty of the wood.

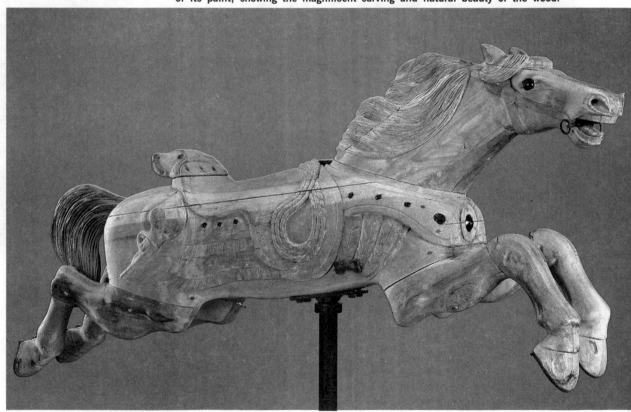

horses with elaborate carved and painted trappings. And as this trend spread to other countries, carousel horses became prime examples of the woodcarver's art.

CAROUSELS IN AMERICA

In the United States, carousels got a boost from the invention of the electric trolley in

As in Europe, the early carousel horses were small and simple. Sometimes they were hung on chains, rather than attached to poles. But as the rides gained popularity, they changed. Carousel horses in the United States developed in three distinct styles. The first, called the Philadelphia style, was started by a carver named Gustav Dentzel,

Carousel horses developed in three styles. This is a fanciful armored horse in the elegant Philadelphia style.

the 1880's. When cities laid the tracks for this new form of public transportation, they extended them beyond populated areas, to allow for future city growth. With transportation so readily available, amusement parks began springing up in the large, vacant parcels of land at the ends of the tracks. And no park, of course, was complete without its carousel.

who moved from Germany to the United States in 1860. Horses made by Dentzel and later carvers who followed his style were elegant and realistic, with great attention to detail.

Charles Looff, a German-born New Yorker, developed a more lavish and fanciful look. It became known as the Coney Island style, named after the most popular amuse-

A lavish jumper in the Coney Island style.

A smaller, simpler horse in the country fair style.

MENAGERIE FIGURES

Not all the creatures carved by carousel makers were horses. From the late 1800's on, riders could choose from a stange assortment of mounts. There were galloping pigs, leaping frogs, and prancing zebras. There were ostriches, rabbits, tigers, camels, deer, lions, bears, and even chickens. These figures were known as menagerie animals.

The carvers didn't stop with animals that people could recognize, either. Some added sea monsters and other mythological creatures. A British maker even produced centaurs with horse bodies and the torsos and heads of famous British soldiers.

Menagerie animals were never as popular as the carousel horses. Perhaps some riders were frightened by the snarling lions and tigers, or perhaps they preferred the romance of a galloping horse to the idea of a galloping chicken. In any case, fewer of these animals were made. Because they are rare today, menagerie animals are considered great prizes by collectors.

ment park in America. His horses galloped and leaped in wild positions, and he added glass jewels and mirrors to their trappings. Looff's carousels were also the first to have electric lights.

The third look was called the country fair style. It featured horses that were much smaller, lighter, and simpler. They were designed for portable carousels that could travel with shows and fairs.

As time went on, the carving on carousel horses became more elaborate. Designers looked to history for inspiration and produced flying arab steeds and armored medieval chargers. Individual carvers added details that left their personal stamp on their works. A few even fitted their horses with real metal horseshoes. But while styles varied, most of the carousel workshops produced their creations in the same way.

The first step in making a carousel horse was to design it, and this was the job of the master carver. Then, following the master's drawings, other carvers would make individual body parts. One might make the legs, while another did the body and a third the neck. (So that it would be lightweight as well as strong, the body was a hollow box, made by sandwiching layers of wood together.) Then the body parts were joined with glue and dowels.

The master carver did the head and the flowing mane himself—these were the most important parts, since they gave the horse its personality. Then any differences in the parts produced by the various carvers would be smoothed out, and the horse would be finished and painted. Leather reins, an upholstered saddle, or a horsehair tail might be added. Often saddles and tails were carved of wood, though, because the fabric and horsehair ones wore out quickly.

The horses were made in several poses. Standers had at least three feet on the ground. Prancers were caught in the act of leaping, with hind feet grounded and front feet in the air. Jumpers had all four feet off the ground, and they moved up and down on their poles as the carousel turned. For timid riders, there were often a few horses pulling chariots with chairlike seats.

All the horses had more decoration on the right side—the side that faced out to the public—than on the left. But the most elaborate carving was reserved for the outer row of horses. And of these, the most beautiful were the king, or lead, horses. They were larger than the others, more heavily decorated, and sometimes bore the name of the carver.

The carousels themselves were beautifully decorated as well. The machinery that turned the ride was hidden with painted and carved panels and with mirrors. Around the outside of the carousel's roof were more panels, often showing portraits of famous people, landscapes, or scenes from mythology. And as the carousel turned, there was always music, provided by a mechanical band organ. Some of the organs produced the sound of more than 100 pipes and horns, together with drums and cymbals.

RESTORED AND COLLECTED

In the early 1900's, there were perhaps 3,000 or 4,000 carousels in the United States and Canada. Carousel makers continued to produce carved wooden horses throughout the 1920's. But then several events—including the Great Depression of the 1930's and World War II—forced many woodcarving shops to close. New carousel animals were mass-produced, stamped out of aluminum or fiberglass. They were still fun to ride, but they were no longer works of art.

Meanwhile, many of the existing carousels were damaged—by neglect, fires, storms, and accidents. Today fewer than 300 of the old-time rides still operate. But many people have come to appreciate their value. Some of the most beautiful have been restored to their former glory. And individual carousel animals are prized by collectors, who are often expert at identifying subtle differences in the styles of the different carvers. The old-fashioned carousel may not be as common as it once was, but it still has its magic.

No carousel was complete without the wonderful tunes of the mechanical band organ—which could often produce the sounds of drums, cymbals, and more than 100 pipes and horns.

Cobalt sea star

STARS OF THE SEA

If you've ever taken a walk along the sea-shore, you may have come upon small animals that look like five-pointed stars. These are sea stars, some of the most colorful and unusual water creatures to be found.

Sea stars live in all the oceans of the world, usually in the shallow waters near the shoreline. They are also known as starfish, but they aren't really fish. They belong to a large group of sea animals called echino-derms, which means "spiny-skinned." Anyone who has ever accidentally stepped on a sea star understands why: The entire surface of the animal's body is covered with hard, sharp spines.

An echinoderm's most important feature is its symmetry (a balanced arrangement). From a central point in its body, identical organs radiate (grow outward), usually in five directions or in multiples of five. Most sea stars have five arms . . . and five eyes (one on the tip of each arm), which sense light. Some sea stars, however, have many arms, and some have no arms at all—although even these types have a radial symmetry.

Blunt-tentacled sea star

Sunflower sea star

Sea stars use their arms for moving and feeding. (The arms are so important, in fact, that if a sea star loses one, it can regrow the lost part.) The undersides of a sea star's arms are covered with hundreds of tiny fingerlike projections called tube feet. At the end of each tube foot is a small suction cup, which the sea star uses to slowly pull itself along the ocean bottom—to attack the clams, oysters, and other shellfish that make up its diet.

A sea star's mouth is in the middle of the underside of its body, and it leads to a large baglike stomach. When a sea star finds a clam or other prey, it wraps its arms around the animal and uses its tube feet to force the shell open. Then the sea star pushes its stomach out of its mouth, right into the body of the clam. Digestive juices from the sea star's stomach break down the clam's tissues. The stomach, with the digested food, is now drawn back into the sea star's body, leaving behind an empty shell.

In addition to sea stars, the echinoderm group includes sea cucumbers, sea urchins, sand dollars, and other creatures. Crinoids —flowerlike animals that have been around for some 500,000,000 years—are the oldest living echinoderms. Feather stars are crinoids, and many of them are extremly beautiful. Some feather stars have as many as 200 delicate arms, which move gracefully back and forth as the animals swim through the water.

Pincushion sea star

Red sea star

UP IN THE AIR

Three brightly colored balls circle in the air above your head, never falling to the ground. The balls fly higher, and you add a fourth, then a fifth. . . . It's the next best thing to magic!

Juggling—the art of tossing and catching objects in the air—is an ancient entertainment that's enjoying new popularity. Any-

where you go, on street corners and in shopping malls, you may be entertained by a juggler. Kids are juggling in schoolyards and on college campuses. Some teachers have even taught juggling to capture their students' interest for more usual subjects.

In some offices, people take juggling breaks instead of coffee breaks. A few doctors and dentists regularly juggle for their patients, to distract them from their fears. There are even special races for "jogglers," who must juggle three balls as they jog.

But the best part about the juggling craze is this: It's not as hard as it looks. People who have learned to juggle say that anyone can do it—all it takes is practice.

AN ANCIENT ART

People and juggling have gone hand-in-hand since ancient times. The earliest jugglers we know about were a troupe of women shown in an ancient Egyptian wall painting. Jugglers were also popular entertainers in ancient Greece. Our word "juggle" comes from the Latin word *joculari,* to joke. The jugglers of the ancient world often combined their fast-paced routines with acrobatics, magic tricks, and other forms of entertainment.

This tradition of combining skills was continued in Europe during the Middle Ages. The masters of juggling at that time were the minstrels and court jesters, who sang and joked as well as juggled. The traveling French entertainers called *jongleurs,* for example, were chiefly minstrels; juggling was a secondary part of their performances.

Jugglers weren't unique to Western countries. Marco Polo saw Asian jugglers when he made his famous journey to China in the 1200's. When the British explorer James Cook visited the South Pacific island of Tonga in the 1700's, he found that the inhabitants were adept at juggling gourds. People juggled in other places, too—in India, Iran, and Japan, to name a few. There were jugglers among the Aztecs and other American Indian groups. And Eskimo women often passed long hours juggling stones. In some early societies, juggling was associated with religious ceremonies.

In Europe and North America, juggling reached new heights as entertainment in the 1800's. At that time, jugglers were featured performers in circuses and vaudeville shows. Balls, plates, and clubs were the objects these jugglers usually tossed, but they used more exotic items too—flaming torches, for example.

There were even juggling specialists. Strong, hefty jugglers specialized in tossing heavy objects such as cannonballs into the air. Equestrian jugglers performed on horseback, often standing on the horse's back as it went around the circus ring. "Salon" jugglers used top hats, canes, bouquets of flowers, and other genteel items in their acts. There were group jugglers, who tossed items back and forth to one another, and jugglers who juggled only with their feet.

Many people think that the greatest juggler who ever lived was Enrico Rastelli (1896–1931). Rastelli set records for juggling the most balls (ten), sticks (eight), and plates (eight). He could also juggle three balls using only his head. The world record for juggling the most objects of all (eleven hoops) was set by Sergei Ignatov, a Russian circus performer. He had to toss the hoops to four times his height to keep them in motion.

JUGGLING BASICS

Experts say that juggling is good for you —it helps develop balance, co-ordination, timing, and concentration. Some psychologists teach it as a way to reduce stress. But many people who try to juggle become frustrated and give up. The reason is usually that they don't know the basic techniques.

Jugglers use several basic tossing patterns. One of the easiest is the cascade, in which the objects are popped from hand to hand in a pattern that looks something like a figure eight turned on its side. A more difficult technique is the shower, in which the objects are kept moving in a circle. Some jugglers use still another method: Rather than tossing objects from hand to hand, they juggle half the objects with one hand and half with the other.

To add more objects, toss higher—the higher an object goes, the longer it takes to come down. Hoops are easier to juggle than balls because you can always catch a hoop by sticking your arm through the middle. Clubs are harder than balls because they have to be caught by the proper end. But experts suggest that you begin with lightweight objects—such as scarves—that fall very slowly.

If you want to get started in juggling, turn the page. Remember, practice makes perfect: Some of the most famous jugglers practiced as much as ten hours a day.

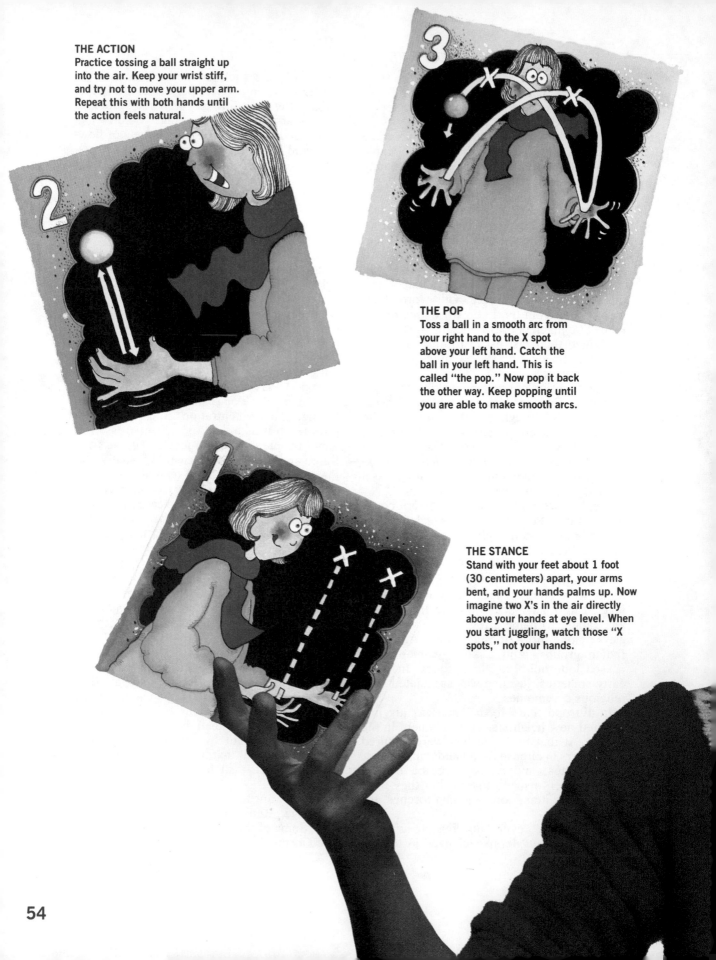

THE ACTION
Practice tossing a ball straight up into the air. Keep your wrist stiff, and try not to move your upper arm. Repeat this with both hands until the action feels natural.

THE POP
Toss a ball in a smooth arc from your right hand to the X spot above your left hand. Catch the ball in your left hand. This is called "the pop." Now pop it back the other way. Keep popping until you are able to make smooth arcs.

THE STANCE
Stand with your feet about 1 foot (30 centimeters) apart, your arms bent, and your hands palms up. Now imagine two X's in the air directly above your hands at eye level. When you start juggling, watch those "X spots," not your hands.

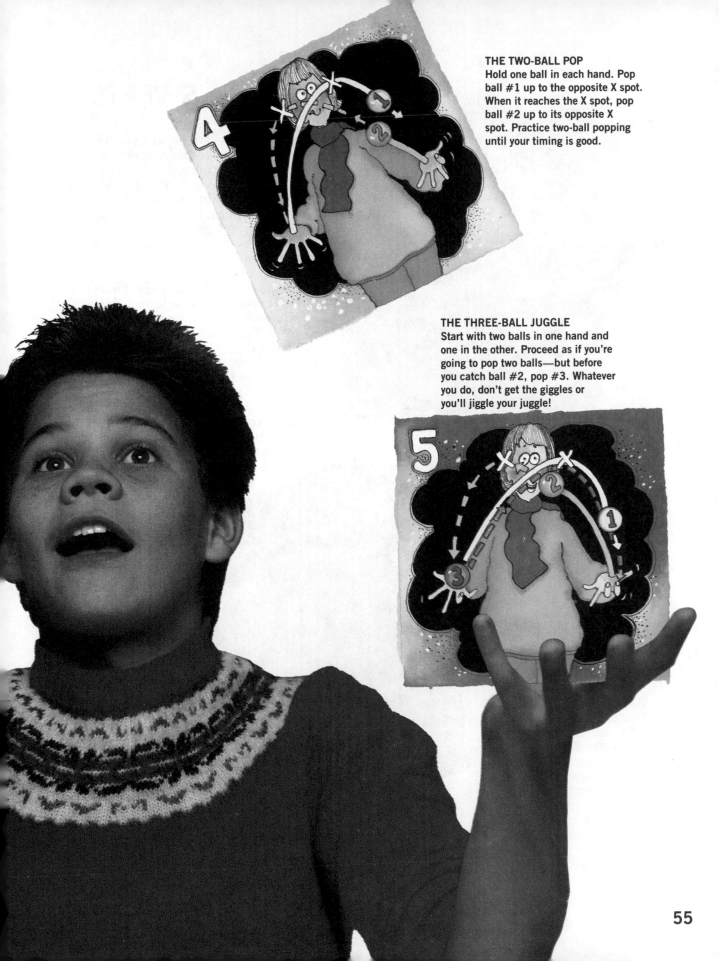

THE TWO-BALL POP
Hold one ball in each hand. Pop ball #1 up to the opposite X spot. When it reaches the X spot, pop ball #2 up to its opposite X spot. Practice two-ball popping until your timing is good.

THE THREE-BALL JUGGLE
Start with two balls in one hand and one in the other. Proceed as if you're going to pop two balls—but before you catch ball #2, pop #3. Whatever you do, don't get the giggles or you'll jiggle your juggle!

SUPER SWEATS

Sweatshirts are IN, and you'll be the envy of everyone in a shirt that you've designed and made yourself. To make one, you'll need a plain sweatshirt in your favorite color; a design; and felt from which to cut the design.

To prevent the felt from shrinking when you wash the shirt, wash the felt in cold water *before* sewing it onto the shirt. Use a towel to remove most of the moisture (don't wring out the felt). Then lay the felt on a flat surface until it's completely dry.

Look for a design you like in books and magazines. Carefully trace it. Use carbon paper to transfer the design to the felt. Cut out the design and sew it onto the shirt. Then add additional decorations, such as sequins and beads.

Lucky Duck. This design involves several pieces of felt that must be carefully pieced together. For such a design, it's best to glue the pieces in place before sewing them to the shirt. Rickrack is added to look like waves. If you're using a long-sleeved shirt, sew additional rows of rickrack above the cuffs.

Witty Kitty. This design uses embroidery to create the features of the cat. When transferring the pattern onto the felt, transfer the features as well as the outline. Use embroidery thread to sew the design onto the shirt. Then embroider the cat's features. You can even embroider a message, such as "I love cats," under the design.

Happy Hands. You don't have to look far for this design! Trace outlines of your hands on a sheet of paper and you have the pattern. For a super gift, trace a friend's hands—without explaining why. Your friend will be delighted when you present this shirt covered with his or her own handprints.

Sweet Hearts. This design was sewn onto the shirt with invisible thread. Another possibility would have been to use embroidery thread in a contrasting color. For a really fashionable look, also decorate a pair of matching sweatpants. Stitch a row of hearts up the side of each leg, or just add one heart under a knee.

IRON MEN,
IRON WOMEN

Imagine swimming 2.4 miles in the ocean. That would be like 77 laps in an Olympic-size pool, only with powerful tides and rolling sea swells to slow you down. Even if you're a fantastic swimmer, it would take you an hour—without stopping.

Tired?

Sorry, there's more. After stumbling ashore, you change into shorts, pull on a T-shirt, and slip into a pair of athletic shoes. Now hop on your bicycle and start pedaling. You've got 112 miles ahead of you! Mountains, valleys, endless flatlands—then more mountains. Five hour, six hours, maybe seven. It's hot and it's muggy.

Don't quit yet! Catch your breath, have a drink of water, and limber up. Now you are going to run a marathon. That's right— 26 miles, 385 yards. At least the sun is going down. If you feel lonely, talk to yourself. If you can't take another step, grit your teeth. Only a few more hours. Keep going, keep going, keep going, keep . . .

Congratulations! You did it! You have just completed your first triathlon!

It sounds impossible. It sounds like madness. But don't tell that to the thousands of supermen and superwomen who take part in triathlon competitions every year. They're very serious about it, and they're in great shape.

The best known of these super-endurance events is the one just described—the Ironman Triathlon World Championship in Hawaii. The competition begins at 7 A.M., and the participants must complete all three legs before midnight. The total distance comes to 140.6 miles—2.4 swimming, 112 bicycling, 26.2 running. Of the 1,018 men and women who began the 1985 Ironman Triathlon, 965 managed to finish, crossing the finish line right up to midnight.

The Hawaii Ironman Championship is not the only triathlon competition. In fact, more than 1,000 similar events are held throughout the United States—from Florida's Gulf Coast Triathlon to San Francisco's Escape from Alcatraz. Foreign competitions include the Nice World Triathlon Championship on the French Riviera. Although most of these races are shorter than Hawaii's Ironman, all of them are incredibly grueling.

HOW IT ALL BEGAN

It was late 1977. On the island of Oahu, Hawaii, a few friends were sitting in a restaurant. They were having a loud but good-natured argument. At the time, Oahu held three separate endurance competitions every year—the 2.4-mile Waikiki Rough Water Swim, the 112-mile Around-Oahu Bike Race, and the Honolulu Marathon. Which was the toughest? Which athletes are in the best physical condition—swimmers, bicycle racers, or distance runners?

The friends never did agree. But one of them came up with an amazing suggestion. Why not combine all three events into one day-long race? And so the triathlon was born.

The first Ironman Championship was held in February, 1978. Only fifteen men took part, but twelve finished. In 1979, fourteen men and one woman participated, and again twelve of them—including the woman, Lyn Lemaire—made it to the end. Then the event began to receive national coverage, and 108 men and women showed up in 1980.

Since that time, the triathlon has become one of the fastest-growing participation sports in America. By 1985 an estimated 250,000 men and women had caught the bug. Several thousand applied for the Ironman alone. (According to the rules, only 1,250 could be accepted.) A number of the competitions are televised, and the sport even has its own magazine—called *Triathlon*. "In a few years," said one triathlete, "this sport will be as big as tennis."

WHAT MAKES THEM GO?

In truth, the triathlon probably never will be as popular as tennis. Almost anybody can step onto a tennis court and knock the ball around for an hour or two. With a few lessons, one can even begin to play matches. To compete in a triathlon, however, one must be in almost superhuman condition. The triathlete must be strong in *three* sports. Each leg of the triathlon is an ordeal, and to combine all three in one day is to push the human body to its limit. Every muscle must be as hard as iron. The mind must be just as tough, always pushing and refusing to give up. The triathlon requires endless training, disciplined eating habits, and great endurance. It is not for everybody.

The best triathletes train 40 or 50 hours every week. That is more time than most people spend at full-time jobs. In fact, many serious triathletes have no time for careers. They rely on prize money (usually meager), product endorsements, their bank accounts, and part-time work. In addition, few of them have much time left for a family life. All in all, there's a lot of sacrifice and a lot of pain.

What makes them do it? One triathlete describes a special feeling that comes with the physical and mental exertion. It is the feeling that "there's no limit to how far you can go." The big payoff, however, is just crossing the finish line—reaching that impossible goal, passing the test of body and spirit.

CHAMPIONS OF CHAMPIONS

Anyone who can muster the strength, determination, and courage to complete a triathlon course is a true champion. But then there are the champions of champions. Among the men, Dave Scott of California has been ranked the world's best. Scott won Hawaii's Ironman four times, and in 1984 his record-setting time was 8 hours, 54 minutes, 20 seconds.

Scott trained extremely hard for his victories. He started every day at 6:30 A.M. First he ran 10 or 15 miles. Then he biked 75 miles. After that, he lifted weights. Finally, to cool off, he swam 3 miles. Sometimes he was at it 55 hours a week.

THE ORDEAL OF JULIE MOSS

The agony of competing in the triathlon and the courage it takes to finish were never more dramatically demonstrated than in a story that emerged from the February, 1982, Ironman Championship. It was the story of a 23-year-old Californian named Julie Moss.

When she plunged into the cool waters of Kailua Bay on the first leg of her ordeal, Moss felt strong. It was early morning, and she swam at a fast, steady pace. One hour and 11 minutes later she completed the 2.4-mile swim, still feeling good.

After showering and changing into biking clothes, she got on her ten-speed and set out on phase two—112 miles under a hot sun. On and on she pedaled, finding new reserves of strength for every hill. After 5 hours and 53 minutes—7 hours total—she finished the bicycle event. Moss was leading but she was exhausted. And there was still the marathon.

She started out slowly, trying to conserve what strength she had left. Every muscle in her body ached. Keep going, keep going, keep going. But now she realized that another woman, 22-year-old Kathleen McCartney, wasn't far behind. Moss kept looking over her shoulder and prayed for the strength to continue. But she was exhausted. She stumbled, regained her balance, and pushed on. Then she fell. An ordinary person would have quit, but Moss wobbled to her feet and kept going.

With less than a mile to go, she was still in front. But she didn't know if she could finish. Again she collapsed. Again she wobbled to her feet and began jogging. Again she dropped, but once more she found a way to go on. With the finish line literally in sight, Julie fell for the last time. The crowd yelled encouragement, but just then McCartney emerged from the darkness and passed her. As McCartney broke the tape, Julie Moss was on her hands and knees, crawling to the finish. Finally she made it—11 hours and 10 minutes after diving into Kailua Bay.

The spirit of it all was summed up by a fellow triathlete: "You just have to hang tough and go for it."

Getting in shape for the triathlon means choosing the right body fuel, and Scott was also on a rigorous diet. A vegetarian, he would eat fifteen pieces of fruit every day, as well as four or five huge salads and all the rice, yogurt, and low-fat cottage cheese he could swallow. Not all triathletes are vegetarians, but you won't find many who eat cookies, cake, or ice cream.

In addition to Dave Scott (who announced his retirement after the 1984 event), other top male triathletes include Scott Tinley, his brother Jeff, and Scott Molina. The 1985 Ironman was won by Scott Tinley, who broke Dave Scott's record with a time of 8 hours, 50 minutes, 54 seconds.

On the women's side, the sport has been dominated by a remarkable pair of twins, Sylviane and Patricia Puntous. Born in Montreal, Canada, the sisters began swimming competitively at age 8, took up running at 16, and entered their first triathlon in 1982. By 1985, the twins between them had won more than a dozen triathlons. In the 1984 Ironman, Sylviane repeated as the women's champion, setting a record of 10 hours, 25 minutes, 13 seconds. The top woman finisher in the 1985 Ironman, however, was Joanne Ernst. She completed the ordeal in a time of only 10 hours, 25 minutes, 22 seconds.

Only!

Getting in shape for the triathlon means eating the right foods. Dave Scott, for years the world's best triathlete, ate enormous amounts of fruit, vegetables, rice, and yogurt every single day that he was in training.

MINNIE'S MAKEOVER

Minnie Mouse and Clarabelle studied the big poster in the school hallway. "Sign up for Tiger Cubs Cheerleader Tryouts," it read.

"I'm going to try out this year," said Minnie firmly. "Mickey will be trying out for the Tiger Cubs football team. This might be one way to get him to notice me."

"You've only got two weeks to get ready for the tryouts," reminded Clarabelle.

"What do you mean, get ready?" asked Minnie.

"Look at the girls who make the squad," said Clarabelle. She began to count off on her fingers.

"First you have to be in great shape."

Minnie looked at her thin legs and round bottom. "I'll join a fitness class," she said.

"Second," said Clarabelle, "you have to be beautiful."

"I'll start a beauty program," Minnie declared firmly.

"And finally," said Clarabelle, "you have to be popular."

Minnie thought for a minute. "I know," she said, "I'll read that book on how to win friends."

Clarabelle wished her friend luck. But she wondered secretly how Minnie would accomplish so much in just two weeks.

Minnie wasted no time putting her self-improvement plan into action. On her way home from school, she enrolled in an afternoon fitness class. Then she stopped at the drug store to pick up a magazine with an article on skin care. And then she was off to the library to check out a book on how to be popular.

The next afternoon Clarabelle stopped by the fitness class to see how her friend was doing.

Minnie was huffing and puffing to keep up with the class. She was kicking her legs high for leg lifts, bending low for knee bends, swinging her arms wide for arm circles, and stretching to reach her toes for sit-ups.

Most of the class moved smoothly and quickly through the exercise routine. But

Minnie barely bumbled through. She was just catching her breath and rubbing her aching legs when Clarabelle found her.

"How's it going?" Clarabelle asked.

"Fine, fine," said Minnie, but she didn't feel quite as confident as she sounded. Getting in shape in such a short time was going to be harder than she had thought.

Clarabelle didn't see her friend again until the next Saturday, when she dropped by Minnie's house. Clarabelle rang the buzzer, and when no one answered, she opened the door slowly and called, "Anyone home?"

"Come in," said Minnie. "I can't get up right now."

Clarabelle gasped when she saw Minnie. She had her elbows soaking in two lemon halves. A large, round cucumber slice covered each eye. Next to her was a bowl of milk.

"What in the world are you doing?" asked Clarabelle.

"It's all right here in this article," said Minnie, pushing the magazine toward her. Clarabelle opened it to a section on skin care. It advised soaking rough elbows in lemons to make them smooth, and putting cucumbers on puffy eyes to relieve redness, and bathing the face in milk.

"This is making me hungry," said Clarabelle. "Is it all right if I fix a sandwich?"

"Sure," said Minnie. Her stomach gave a growl.

"Would you like one?" asked Clarabelle.

"No," said Minnie. "I'm on a fitness diet. I can have half a cup of skim milk in another hour."

Clarabelle really hoped Minnie would make the cheerleading squad. She was trying so hard.

The next time Clarabelle saw Minnie she was walking across the school yard with her nose in a book.

"Hi, Minnie," she called, and she ran to catch up with her friend.

"I'm almost through with this book on how to be popular," said Minnie. "Now I have to practice. It says when you meet someone to start with a smile and a warm 'hello.' "

Just then the girls saw Mickey Mouse coming across the grass.

"Hello, Mickey," Minnie beamed, with her biggest, widest smile.

"Hello," said Mickey slowly. "Are you feeling okay?"

"Why, yes," said Minnie. "Why do you ask?"

"You're smiling kinda funny. Do your teeth hurt?" he asked. Then he snapped his fingers. "Of course, you've just been to the dentist. Your teeth look great! See ya."

"Thanks, Mickey," Minnie said.

Clarabelle tried to change the subject. "Only five days until the tryouts," she reminded. "I probably won't see you until then. Good luck."

On the morning of the tryouts, Minnie woke up early, brimming with confidence. She pulled on the new outfit she had bought specially for the day and plopped down in front of the mirror.

Then very carefully, just like they do in the beauty magazines, she applied several layers of super-lavish lash-builder mascara. She drew on a smooth line of New Wave Red Lip Creme and puffed on Spice Mist face powder.

Stepping back from the mirror, Minnie turned first one way, and then the other. She winked at her reflection. It had been a rough two weeks, but today she was ready to make the team.

At the morning tryouts, all the girls waited together on a bench, chattering and giggling. Finally the girls' coach arrived. She had each girl draw a slip of paper out of a hat. Each piece had a number on it. Minnie's was five—she would be fifth in line to do her routine.

"Number one," the coach called.

The first girl glanced down at a piece of paper she'd been studying. Taking a pair of pompoms, she put the paper down and took her place facing the coach and the girls on the bench. She moved effortlessly through the routine, using her hands, arms, and legs in time to the cheer.

"Very good," said the coach. "We'll let you know in a few days." The girl came back to the bench smiling and out of breath. She picked up her books and left for class.

"Number two," called the coach. The next girl was also studying a sheet of paper. When she put it down to do the routine, Minnie reached for it. She had a terrible sinking feeling when she realized what it was. On the paper were three cheers and illustrated movements to match the routine.

In all her efforts to make the squad, Minnie realized that she had overlooked the most important thing of all: practicing the routine!

She sat numbly on the bench as numbers three and four were called. Then the coach called her number—"Five!"

Minnie did the best she could, trying to remember what the other girls had done.

"Push 'em back, push 'em back, 'wa-a-ay back!'' she said, pushing her pompoms out in front. Then she kicked high in the air and yelled, "Yay, Tiger Cubs!''

"You can stop now, Minnie,'' said the coach. "I'd like you to wait on the bench until after the tryouts.''

Minnie dragged herself over to the bench and sat down to wait. She knew she hadn't made the team. No one else had been stopped in the middle of a routine and told to wait on the bench. She just hoped she wasn't in some kind of trouble.

At last the coach came over. "Your routine wasn't good enough to earn you a place on the squad this year,'' she said gently. "You have another year to practice for next year's cheerleading tryouts. But I have another position for you on the squad. You'd be perfect for it.''

Minnie could hardly believe her ears.

"What is it?'' she said, barely able to wait for an answer.

"We need two people, a boy and girl, to be the team mascots. And you're just the right size for the tiger cub costume. Would you like the job?''

"Oh, yes!'' gasped Minnie. "I'd love it!''

"It will take a lot of time,'' cautioned the coach. "It means lots of practice with the boy playing the other part.''

"Oh, that's just fine with me,'' beamed Minnie. "And by the way, who is the other mascot?''

"Here he comes now,'' said the coach. "He was too short to make the football team.''

Minnie turned to see Mickey Mouse coming across the field. He waved when he saw her and smiled. "Hi, partner!'' said Mickey. "Welcome to the Tiger Cubs!''

WITCH-FUL THINKING

"Bubble, bubble, toil and trouble, fire burn and cauldron bubble," chant the three witches in Shakespeare's play *Macbeth*. As they chant, they whip up a brew of newts' eyes, frogs' toes, and other unappetizing ingredients.

Like other witches in story and legend, these three hags are dabblers in the supernatural. Through charms, spells, and potions, they can call up spirits and perform magic. A witch may be good or bad, practicing white magic or black. But in most stories, witches are evil—something to be feared. The word "witch" comes from the Old English word *wicce,* meaning a sorceress. Men who practice magic are sometimes called wizards or warlocks, but often the term "witch" is used for both sexes.

WITCHES IN HISTORY

The power to call up spirits was common to witches in many times and places. It was said that witches had many other powers, too. They could make crops wither in the field and make milk cows go dry. They could call up storms, make milk go sour, and keep cream from being churned into butter. They took horses from people's barns at night and rode them to the point of exhaustion. They could fly through the air on broomsticks. They could change themselves or others into animals. They might use their knowledge of herbs and potions to help people, but more often they brewed potions that would cause disease and even death to anyone who offended them. And witches were often surrounded by familiars—cats, hares, or other animals that were said to embody the spirits of demons.

Where did witches get such powers? In early Christian times, it was believed that they sold their souls to the Devil or to some pagan god in exchange for the ability to perform magic. Covens, or groups, of witches were said to gather to worship their masters in the Black Mass, an imitation of the Roman Catholic Mass. These services were held four times a year on the witches' sabbaths—Candlemas (February 2), May Eve (April 30), Lammas (August 1), and All Hallows' Eve (October 31).

Naturally, church and government were opposed to witchcraft. Witchcraft was banned in Europe during the Middle Ages, and anyone found guilty of practicing it was put to death. A mole or a birthmark might count as evidence of a pact with the Devil. Or a suspected witch might be tied up and thrown into water. If she floated, she was guilty; if she sank, she was innocent. These laws were carried to the New World, and in the mid-1600's several hundred people in Massachusetts and Connecticut were accused of being witches. In one town, Salem Village, twenty suspected witches were hanged.

There is, of course, no evidence that any human being ever attained the magical powers that witches were said to have. Most likely, the stories began out of misunderstanding. A farmer didn't understand the natural causes of a hailstorm that ruined his crop, for example, so he blamed it on witchcraft—a neighbor or someone in the next town had cast a spell and called up the hailstorm. Often the victim of such gossip was an old woman who lived alone.

Belief in witches died out in the 1700's, as scientists began to find explanations for diseases and many other calamities. But tales of witchcraft lingered on, and today witches play an important part in many stories and legends.

WITCHES IN STORIES

Stories of witches and the magic they perform have been around a long time. Witches are mentioned in the Bible. In the Book of Samuel, Saul, the king of Israel, banned witchcraft and wizardry. But later he visited a witch and asked her to call up the spirit of the prophet Samuel. At first the witch was afraid that Saul was trying to trick her, but then she did as she was asked. The spirit of Samuel appeared and foretold that Israel would be defeated in battle by the Philistines, and that Saul would be killed. And this was in fact what happened.

Ancient Greek tales also told of witches. Hecate was the Greek goddess of sorcery and witchcraft. She was said to haunt grave-yards and crossroads, and when dogs barked at night it was thought that they were warning that Hecate was near. The most famous Greek witch was Circe. Like many Greek witches—but unlike most in tales from other lands—Circe was a beautiful woman. According to the story told in Homer's *Odyssey,* when the hero Ulysses visited her island she enchanted him and changed his companions into animals.

Nearly every part of the world has its own stories of witches. A Finnish tale tells how Vainamöinen, the good wizard who befriended the Finnish people, tricked Louhi, an evil witch who sent darkness and plagues from the north. It seems that Louhi had a magic mill that ground unlimited supplies of gold and grain. The wizard resolved to have it, and he sailed to Louhi's land with a company of men. When he arrived, he played his harp and sang, putting Louhi and all her soldiers and animals into a deep trance. Then he took the mill and sailed for home.

Louhi, naturally, was furious when she awoke. First she sent a deep fog that surrounded the wizard's ship, so that the pilot couldn't steer. But the wizard cut through the fog with his magic sword, and the ship sailed on. Then Louhi herself appeared—in the form of a huge sea bird that perched on the ship's mast. She spread her wings and threatened to destroy the ship and its crew. But the wizard fought her off, and she flew home wounded to her own dark lands.

One of the most famous witches of all time is Baba Yaga, who figures in many Russian folktales. She lived in a clearing deep in the forest, and her house was strange indeed. It sat on top of an immense chicken leg, so it could hop around in circles to keep intruders out. The fence that surrounded the clearing was made of human bones—for, like many legendary witches, Baba Yaga would kill and eat any unfortunate people who wandered into her clearing. When she went out, she rode through the sky in a mortar, using a pestle to row the air and a broom to sweep her tracks behind her.

Witches abound in other European folk and fairy tales. You probably remember the witch in *Hansel and Gretel*. In this story,

two children, Hansel and Gretel, are abandoned by their parents in the forest. They wander until they find a witch's house—made of bread and roofed with cakes, with windows of transparent sugar. When the hungry children start to nibble, the witch pops out and lures them inside. Soon they are her prisoners; her plan is to cook them and eat them.

First, though, she decides she must fatten Hansel, so she locks him in a stable and puts Gretel to work bringing him meals. But Hansel tricks her—this witch, like many, is nearsighted. When she asks Hansel to hold out his finger so that she can see if he is fat, he holds out a bone instead. Finally she decides to eat the children, thin or fat, and heats up her oven. But Gretel tricks her, too. She gets the witch to stick her head inside the oven, shoves her in, and slams the door. It's the witch herself who bakes, while the children run home safely with her jewels.

Not all witches are so easily tricked, as can be seen in the fairy tale *Rapunzel*. In this tale, a man sneaks into a witch's garden to steal vegetables for his wife, who is expecting a long-wanted child. The witch catches him and strikes a bargain with him: She will let him live if he gives her the child.

The child is a girl named Rapunzel. The witch takes her and locks her in a tower with no door—just one window, high in the air. Rapunzel grows into a beautiful woman, but no one sees her except the witch. When the witch wants to come up, she tells Rapunzel to let down her long golden braids from the window, and then the witch climbs up the hair.

As you might expect, one day a prince wanders into the forest and happens on this scene. After the witch leaves, he asks Rapunzel to let down her hair again so that he can climb up. She does, and they fall in love and agree to be married. But when the witch finds out, she is furious. She cuts off Rapunzel's long locks and sends her away, deep in the wilderness. Then the prince returns, and the witch hangs out the cut-off braids for him. When he climbs up and learns what has happened to his love, he despairs and leaps out the window. He isn't killed, but he lands in thorns that scratch out his eyes. Still, the story ends happily. After the prince wanders around blind for a few years, he finds Rapunzel. Her tears fall on his eyes and cure his blindness.

A less well-known story, *The Water Lily,* tells of a witch at work. In this tale three girls live with an old hag—the witch—in a cottage in the woods. They spend their days spinning gold thread, and the witch won't permit them to speak to any man.

But the youngest of the three falls in love with a prince and runs off with him. In revenge, the witch casts a spell. She takes nine kinds of enchanter's nightshade (a plant) and some salt (which she first bewitches) and puts it in a cloth, which she rolls into the shape of a ball. Then she tosses the ball after the couple, saying:

Whirlwind—mother of the wind!
Lend thy aid 'gainst her who sinned!
Carry with thee this magic ball.
Cast her from his arms forever,
Bury her in the rippling river.

The ball strikes the two just as they are crossing a
bridge. They fall into the water, and the girl is changed
into a water lily. But this tale, too, has a happy ending:
The prince enlists the aid of a wizard from Finland, who
tells him how to break the witch's spell.

Not all stories of witches come to us from long ago and
far away. Witches as well as a wizard are important characters in *The Wonderful Wizard of Oz,* which was written
by L. Frank Baum in 1900. The story begins with a cy-
clone that carries Dorothy, together with her home and
dog, from Kansas to the Land of Oz. There she meets
both good and evil witches. In fact, Dorothy's house
lands on a wicked witch, killing her. Later Dorothy is
captured and held prisoner by another witch—the
Wicked Witch of the West. If Dorothy is ever to return
to Kansas, she must kill this witch. Eventually she does
the deed by accident—she douses the witch with a pail
of water, and the evil hag melts away before her eyes.

In *Oz,* as in other tales, wicked witches don't get their
way; good always triumphs in the end!

FAR-OUT FROGS

All frogs have certain characteristics in common. They have moist, smooth skin . . . two bulging eyes . . . four legs . . . and no tail. But this basic body plan is just a starting point: These amphibians (animals that live both on land and in water) have unique physical features that make them some of the most diverse creatures in the animal kingdom. The differences among species of frogs help each to adapt to its own particular environment.

INVISIBLE . . . OR VERY VISIBLE

Many frogs take on the coloring of their surroundings, blending in so perfectly that insects and other small prey remain unaware of their presence until it's too late. Frogs that live high in trees have a bright green color. Those that live in the undergrowth of a forest are often a light, olive green, with dark green

or black spots. Those that live among leaves on the forest floor are shades of brown. Some frogs can even change the color of their skin as they move from light to dark surroundings.

Still other frogs are brightly colored—this provides no camouflage but does serve a different purpose. Many brightly colored frogs have skin glands that secrete a powerful poison. The colors seem to serve as a warning, telling would-be predators to stay away. The arrow poison frogs of Central and South America produce a poison that quickly affects the nerves of an enemy, causing it to lose control of its muscles. The poison is so effective, it is used by local Indians on the tips of their arrows.

Often, you need to know something about a frog's habits to appreciate the importance of its coloring. The tiny red-eyed tree frog of

Central America has, as you might guess, bright red eyes. It also has patches of bright blue coloring on the inside of its legs and underside of its body—coloring that is certainly obvious during daylight hours. But this frog is active only at night. When it sleeps during the day, it tucks its legs in and shows only green skin that blends with its surroundings. Still, it's always possible that a sharp-eyed predator might spot the frog. If so, the frog will flash its bright blue coloring, startling the enemy and giving the frog a chance to escape.

LEGS, LUNGS, NOSES

Most frogs have two powerful hind legs that enable them to leap quickly out of harm's way. But the creeping frogs of Central and South America have comparatively weak hind legs. So when danger threatens, they have an unusual alternative to jumping —they arch their backs, stretch out their legs with the bottoms of their feet turned up, and pretend they're dead.

The gliding frogs of Asia have webs between their toes. Spreading the webs wide, they can easily escape predators by gliding from one branch of a tree to another.

Most frogs have long, sticky tongues, which can be flicked out like whips. The African clawed frog, however, has no tongue —and doesn't seem to need one. Unlike

Many frogs that are brightly colored, such as these arrow poison frogs, have skin glands that secrete a powerful poison. Thus their bright colors seem to serve as a warning, telling enemies to keep away.

most frogs, this frog lives only in water. It uses its sharp claws to dig insects out of the mud, and then pushes them into its mouth with its legs.

The barking frog of the United States—so-named because its call sounds much like a dog's bark—puffs itself up with air when threatened. Its enemy often backs off, not willing to attack such a large, fearsome beast.

When the spatulate-nosed frog is threatened, it just pops into a convenient hole. Then it plugs up the opening with its large, spatula-shaped head.

RAISING THEIR YOUNG

Most frogs aren't very good parents. They lay their eggs in water, then leave. Before the eggs can develop into tadpoles, many are eaten by predators or die when the water evaporates. But some species of frogs provide additional care for their eggs.

Glass frogs of Central America lay eggs on leaves hanging over streams. The eggs are surrounded by a jellylike covering that keeps them damp. Often, a glass frog parent will guard the eggs and keep them moist with water from its bladder. When the eggs hatch and the tadpoles have developed enough to swim, they drop into the water below.

In some species, the eggs are carried by a parent until they hatch. Female marsupial frogs carry their eggs in pouchlike structures

The gliding frog of Asia (*above*) spreads its webbed toes and escapes predators by gliding from one tree branch to another. The glass frog of Central America (*below*) guards its eggs, which are surrounded by a jellylike substance.

A male Darwin's frog swallows eggs into his huge vocal sac. They develop into froglets and jump, fully formed, out of his mouth (*above*). The spatulate-nosed frog (*below*) can escape into a hole and plug it up with its spatula-shaped head.

on their backs. In one species, the female carries the eggs until the tadpoles have developed. She then heads for water, where she flexes her body, causing the pouch to open so that the tadpoles can leave and swim away. In another species, the female carries the young until they have turned into fully developed frogs. Only then does the pouch open, enabling as many as 40 tiny frogs to push their way out into the world.

Some frog fathers get into the act, too. The female arrow poison frog lays its eggs on damp ground. When the young hatch, they wiggle onto their father's back. And he becomes a walking nursery until the babies are old enough to swim. Another South American frog, the female Darwin's frog, lays her eggs on land, where they are guarded by several males for about two weeks. Then each male swallows a few of the eggs, letting them slide down into his huge vocal sac. There, the eggs hatch into tadpoles, which grow and gradually develop into froglets. They then jump one by one, fully formed, out of the father's mouth.

The parental habits of the Darwin's frog are indeed unusual. But the next time you see a frog in your garden or beside a quiet pond, don't dismiss it as a dull, uninteresting creature. It, too, has habits that are ''far out.''

COMPACT DISCS: MUSIC BY NUMBERS

Imagine being at home and listening to music that sounds so rich and pure, it's almost as if an orchestra were playing right in the middle of your living room. This is what compact discs provide. Compact discs are the newest way to record and play music. They are becoming so popular that they may eventually make phonograph records and tapes obsolete.

A compact disc, or CD, looks somewhat like a phonograph record—it's round and flat and has a hole in the middle. But that's where the similarities end. A phonograph record is made of dark vinyl plastic; a CD is made of shiny aluminum sandwiched between two layers of clear plastic. A record is played on both sides; a CD is played on only one side. A CD is smaller than an LP record, but it can hold up to one and a half times as much music.

But the compact disc system is truly unique because of the technologies used to record and play the music: (1) Phonograph records and tapes are analog recordings. On compact discs, music is recorded digitally. (2) A record is played on a turntable that uses a needle to "read" the music, and a tape is played on a machine that uses a magnetic head. A CD is played on a machine that uses a laser to "read" the music.

CD RECORDING

Understanding analog and digital recording may be easier if you think of how the terms relate to clocks. An analog clock is one with hands that move smoothly around the clock's face—"copying" the passage of time. On such a clock it's easy to note when an hour has passed, but often difficult to note precisely when one second has passed.

A digital clock "slices up" time into tiny bits. It's easy to note seconds, as they are flashed on the face of the clock.

In an analog recording, sound waves are "copied." The sound waves are converted into electrical impulses that cause a recording needle to cut grooves in a record, or that form magnetic patterns on a tape.

In a digital recording, the sound waves are "sliced up" into tiny pieces. Each piece of sound is given a 16-digit number, composed entirely of ones and zeros. The number indicates the frequency and level of that bit of sound. All the numbers are then recorded on the aluminum layer of the compact disc as billions of microscopic pits. It is this "music by numbers" aspect of digital recordings that makes them different from other types of recordings.

Just as digital timepieces are more precise than analog timepieces, a digital recording is more precise than an analog recording. Each *bit* of sound is so exactly defined that it can't be left out or distorted.

CD PLAYERS

A special player is needed to play a compact disc. The player contains a tiny laser. As a disc is played, a beam of light from the laser hits the aluminum layer of the disc and "reads" the 16-digit code numbers from the microscopic pits. The player changes these numbers into electrical impulses, which are, in turn, changed into sound waves.

As with record and cassette players, CD players come in many sizes, styles, and prices. There are home, portable, and automobile systems. The home CD player can be connected to a regular stereo system and speakers.

CD ADVANTAGES

Because the laser never actually touches the disc (as a needle touches a record, and a magnetic head touches a tape), there is almost no wear on the disc. You can play the disc a thousand times and it will sound as good as when you first bought it. In comparison, records and many tapes gradually wear out. Records can be scratched, and cassette tapes can be mangled and split. But the sound pits on the compact disc are protected by the clear plastic layers. Other things you won't hear on a CD are the hissing sounds and distortion that may occur when records and tapes are played.

A greater range of sounds can be recorded on compact discs than on records and tapes. That's why music on a CD system in your home will sound much more like live music. In fact, some people say that CD sound can be *too* good. Sometimes you may hear the musicians breathing!

Will compact discs really replace records and tapes? Someday, perhaps, but not for a long time. While CD's have music for every taste, only about 4,000 titles are currently available. This is compared with the more than 50,000 titles that are available on records and tapes. And CD's are more expensive than records and tapes (although prices keep dropping).

Certainly people who have lots of records and tapes will keep them and continue to play them—but many will also buy compact discs, to enjoy those fantastic digital sounds.

LAUGHTER: INNER EXERCISE

"Laughter is the best medicine" is an old saying—and it's one that may contain more than a grain of truth. You know that it feels good to laugh. But did you know that laughter can actually make you a happier and healthier person? At least, that's what some scientists have recently concluded after studying the physical and mental effects of laughter. They even have a name for this branch of scientific study—gelotology, from the Greek word for laughter, *gelos*.

WHAT IS LAUGHTER?

Gelotology can't tell a comedian which jokes will make an audience laugh. But it has turned up some interesting facts about laughter. For example, humans are the only animals that have the ability to laugh at something that strikes them as funny. Chimpanzees and some other apes can laugh, but only when they're tickled.

Human babies start to laugh when they're about 10 weeks old. By the time they're 4 months old, they're laughing about once an hour. And 4-year-old children laugh as often as every four minutes. The average adult laughs fifteen times a day, with each laugh lasting anywhere from half a second to a minute. But an especially cheery soul may laugh as many as 400 times in the course of a day. And as you've probably noticed, laughter is contagious—if one person in your classroom cracks up, the others are likely to follow suit.

Everyone's laugh is different. Yours may be a cackle or a roar. Your chest capacity and vocal power help determine how you laugh, along with a lot of other factors. Most people's laughs get deeper as they get older. Eventually, though, vocal cords become less elastic. This is why elderly people often have very high-pitched laughs.

What, exactly, happens when you laugh? Almost every part of your body is involved. First, you see or hear something that strikes you as funny—a cartoon, a joke, your kitten doing a somersault. Immediately, your brain sends signals along nerves throughout your body. Some of the signals stimulate glands to produce body chemicals such as epinephrine. These chemicals make you more alert, and they stimulate your heart and lungs to work faster. They also cause your arteries to contract, so your blood pressure starts to go up.

At the same time, your muscles are getting into the act. Your face muscles contract, drawing your features into a grimace. Your lips are pulled back, and your nostrils are flared. Your stomach and chest muscles tighten. Your diaphragm, the sheet of muscle between your lungs and abdomen that contracts when you inhale, tenses. Air starts to build up in your lungs. Meanwhile, the muscles that control your vocal cords go into spasms, and you can't speak.

Suddenly your stomach and chest muscles contract in a spasm, forcing the air out of your lungs—as fast as 70 miles (113 kilometers) an hour. It rushes past your vocal cords in a roar of laughter, while tear glands release tears from your eyes.

The body chemicals that were released when you started laughing also prompt you to keep laughing, which is why once you start to laugh you sometimes feel as if you'll never stop. And as your heart keeps working harder, increasing your circulation, your face gets red and your temperature may go up half a degree. While all this is going on, though, your leg muscles are starting to feel weak. You collapse on the closest chair, gasping for air.

As the laughing fit ends, your muscles start to relax. Gradually your blood pressure and your heart rate drop—in fact, they drop below normal, a sign of relaxation and reduced stress.

Laughter may make you a happier, healthier person. Have you heard the one about . . . ?

TEACHER: "Rich, I can hardly read your handwriting. You have to learn to write more clearly."
RICH: "Aw, what's the use? If I wrote any clearer, you'd only complain about my spelling!"

What did Nancy say when the English teacher asked her to name two pronouns? *Who me?*

Are you Hungary?
Yes, Siam.
Okay, I'll Fiji a baked Alaska cooked in Greece.

What is light as air but can't be held for long? *Your breath.*

What did one eye say to the other eye? *Just between you and me, something smells.*

MOTHER: "Now Elizabeth, don't you know you aren't supposed to eat with your knife?"
ELIZABETH: "I know, Mom, but my fork leaks."

When you lose something, why do you always find it in the last place you look? *Because you stop looking as soon as you find it.*

BILL: "Is it bad luck to have a cat follow you?"
PHIL: "It depends. Are you a man or a mouse?"

What animal took the most luggage into the Ark, and what animal took the least? *The elephant took a trunk, and the rooster had only a comb.*

FATHER: "At your age I could name all the presidents—and in proper order, too."
SON: "Yes, but there were only three or four of them then."

How can you lift an elephant? *Put an acorn underneath him and wait fifty years.*

BABY CELERY: "Mama, where did I come from?"
MOTHER CELERY: "Hush, dear. The stalk brought you."

Why do bumblebees hum? *They know the tune but not the words.*

MOTHER: "Mary, if you eat the rest of that cake, you'll burst."
MARY: "Okay. Pass the cake and get out of the way!"

LAUGHTER MAY KEEP YOU HEALTHY

The effects of laughter on your body are a lot like the effects of exercise. In fact, some scientists say that laughter is inner exercise —it vibrates through your whole body and gives a good workout to the muscles of your chest and stomach, as well as to your diaphragm. And the increases in your heart rate and respiration help strengthen your heart and lungs, in the same way that jogging does.

The good effects of laughter go on long after the chuckling stops. Your muscles are more relaxed than they were before you laughed. Because blood pressure and heart rate drop below normal after laughter, the heart is less stressed than it was before. And just as in jogging, the muscular effort involved in laughing burns calories. There is also some evidence that a good laugh prompts the stomach to secrete enzymes that aid digestion. Some scientists think that laughter may even be good for your liver.

A case of the giggles has other effects, too. Some studies show that the right side of the brain, believed to be the creative side, is more active when people laugh. And in addition to the chemicals that make you alert and speed your pulse and respiration, nerve impulses may also stimulate the release of other body chemicals, called endorphins and enkephalins. These chemicals dull feelings of pain and produce a general allover glow of well-being.

There are psychological benefits as well as physical ones. Laughter distracts you from things that may be worrying or upsetting you. It can relieve stress and pressure, and it can make you feel less anxious in tense situations. In fact, scientists think that laughter may have developed as a way of dealing with just such situations—by providing an outlet for tension and fear.

Is it possible to "die laughing"? Yes, although it's not possible to "split your sides." A few people who have suffered from circulatory diseases have actually had strokes because they laughed too hard. But this is very rare.

LAUGHTER AS MEDICINE

If your doctor prescribes your favorite comic book the next time you're down with the flu, he or she won't be coming up with

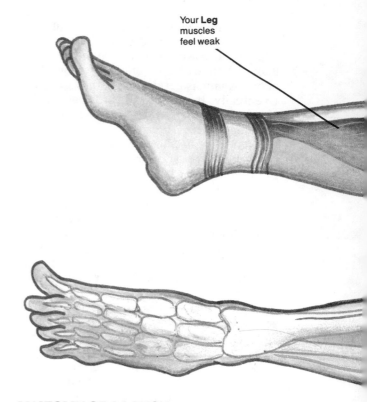

Your **Leg** muscles feel weak

ANATOMY OF A LAUGH

anything new. In the 1400's, a surgeon named Henri de Mondeville told jokes to his patients as they left the operating room, to speed their recovery. In the 1700's, Richard Mulcaster, an English educator, advised tickling under the armpits as a treatment for colds and melancholy. And in at least one North American Indian tribe, the Ojibwa, medicine men performed tricks and stunts to make their patients laugh away their illnesses.

Today, doctors are giving new weight to the idea of laughter as medicine. Laughter seems to help all kinds of medical problems —headaches, infections, arthritis, and high blood pressure among them. People with the respiratory condition known as emphysema, who have difficulty breathing, find that a fit of laughing helps clear their lungs, and they breathe more freely. Laughter can also act like an anesthetic, lessening pain.

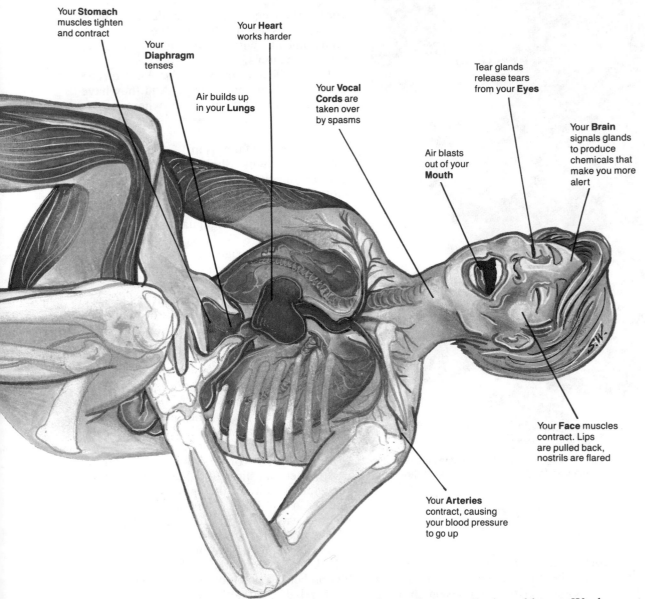

Your **Stomach** muscles tighten and contract

Your **Diaphragm** tenses

Air builds up in your **Lungs**

Your **Heart** works harder

Your **Vocal Cords** are taken over by spasms

Tear glands release tears from your **Eyes**

Air blasts out of your **Mouth**

Your **Brain** signals glands to produce chemicals that make you more alert

Your **Face** muscles contract. Lips are pulled back, nostrils are flared

Your **Arteries** contract, causing your blood pressure to go up

People who work with the mentally ill have found that a good dose of laughter can act like a tranquilizer and can even help bring seriously disturbed people back in touch with reality. In some prisons, inmates try to straighten out through a program that uses cartoon humor to help them understand their problems.

Cards, books, records, and movies are being used in hospitals and centers for the elderly to help people feel better and recover faster from medical problems. Workers at these facilities find that when people laugh, they feel less depressed and less panicky about their illnesses. One nurse was so impressed with the effects of laughter that she founded a group to promote humor in hospitals—the NFL, or Nurses for Laughter.

Laughter will never replace medicine, of course. And getting sick isn't a joke—you won't be able to just laugh off the flu. But clearly, a good laugh can't hurt, and it may even make you a happier, healthier person. No kidding!

Koko the gorilla plays gently with her kitten Lips, and she often uses the sign for "baby" when she is cradling him.

ANIMAL TALK

A gorilla that asks for a pet kitten, and then gives the cat a name? A chimpanzee that tells its keeper what television shows it wants to watch? It sounds impossible, but it's true.

For many years, people have pointed to the ability to use language as one of the greatest differences between humans and animals. While animals communicate in simple ways, only humans seem able to use words as symbols. And only humans seem able to communicate complicated, abstract thoughts.

Now new research is casting doubt on that belief. In several studies, scientists have taught members of the ape family to use language. The apes can't speak—their vocal cords aren't equipped to handle the sounds we use in speech. But they've learned to communicate with their human teachers through symbols.

Two of the apes in the studies have turned out to be exceptional pupils. And they have won the hearts of people everywhere.

KOKO

Koko became famous in 1985 as the gorilla who loves kittens. She's also the star of the longest ongoing ape language study. For more than thirteen years, she's been taught to communicate through American Sign Language, the hand language used by deaf people. Today Koko regularly uses more than 500 different signs.

Koko, who lives in a compound near San Francisco, can ask her human teachers to give her her favorite foods and to play her favorite games. She enjoys picture books—especially books about gorillas. (When asked what her favorite animal is, she always signs "gorilla.") She can identify many objects and name many activities. And when she comes across something new, she sometimes makes up a sign for it—for a ring, for example, she signed "finger bracelet." She's even discussed such abstract concepts as death with her teachers.

But Koko's favorite subject seems to be cats. When she first told her teachers that she wanted a kitten, they gave her a toy cat. She wasn't pleased. Then a litter of three kittens was brought to the compound. "Love that," Koko signed. She picked out a tailless male and named him All Ball.

Koko played gently with Ball, cradling him on her leg as a mother gorilla would cradle her baby. Sometimes she even dressed him up in linen napkins. When the kitten nipped her, she signed, "Obnoxious cat."

Then Ball was killed by a car. When Koko was told, she gave a gorilla cry and signed, "Sad." But in March, 1985, Koko got a new kitten, another tailless male. She was delighted. She named her new pet Lips, maybe because its bright pink nose reminded her of lipstick. A few months later she got a second kitten, which she named Smoky. Now Koko has a double distinction: She's one of the few apes that can communicate with humans. And she's probably the only one that keeps cats as pets.

KANZI

In most of the ape language studies, researchers have spent years painstakingly teaching the animals how to use the most basic symbols. But Kanzi, a four-year-old pygmy chimpanzee at a research center near Atlanta, Georgia, took researchers by surprise. He seems to pick up symbols spontaneously, the same way that human children learn. And he also has a great understanding of words people speak.

Instead of sign language, Kanzi uses a group of 250 symbols on a keyboard. When he wants to say something, he presses the appropriate keys. His first exposure to the keyboard came when he was an infant. He spent many hours in a laboratory where researchers were trying to teach his mother (who had been born in the wild) to use the signs. At the age of 2½, Kanzi suddenly began to use some of the symbols himself—without ever having been taught.

Today Kanzi can request to go places or do things, comment on what he does or what others do, and ask to play games of chase and hide-and-seek with his teachers. He's also learned some new words through a special television show—an ape version of "Sesame Street" that shows objects together with their symbols. Kanzi has even figured out on his own how to ask to see his favorite television shows—by pushing the buttons for "TV" and "campfire," for example, he asks to see the movie *Quest for Fire*.

Kanzi also seems to understand many more spoken words than do other apes that have been studied. He can even respond to fairly complicated requests. When a teacher asked him to get a diaper for his infant sister Mulika, for example, he went and got the diaper and took it to his sister. (Mulika herself has begun to play with the keyboard, but so far her vocabulary is limited to "milk.")

Researchers say that Kanzi's language skills are exceptional and very humanlike. Is Kanzi unique in his language abilities, or can other apes learn to communicate as he does? The researchers don't know. Kanzi is the first pygmy chimpanzee to be studied in depth. Some researchers think that other pygmy chimpanzees may share his talent: Of all the apes, that species is thought to be the closest to humans.

Both pygmy chimpanzees and gorillas are rare—in fact, they're in danger of becoming extinct. If people can truly teach them to communicate, we can learn much about their world. The ape language studies have other benefits, too. By studying how apes learn, we may find out more about how humans learn. The techniques developed in the ape language studies have already been used to help teach mentally handicapped children, with good success.

Instead of sign language, pygmy chimpanzee Kanzi "talks" by using geometric symbols on a keyboard. Researchers say that Kanzi's language skills are exceptional and very humanlike.

P. T. BARNUM: THE GREAT SHOWMAN
An Anniversary Album

When people think of the circus, one name springs to mind: Barnum. Phineas Taylor Barnum probably did more to make the circus into the wondrous attraction we know than any other person. And 1985 marked the 175th anniversary of his birth.

P. T. Barnum was born on July 5, 1810, in Bethel, Connecticut. As a young man, he sold hats and groceries in New York City. But in 1835, his life changed. He heard of a slave woman who was said to have been George Washington's nurse. Barnum bought her and put her on display, claiming she was 161 years old. (In fact, she was 80 and had never met Washington.) Such exploits launched his career as a showman—and his hoaxes earned him the title Prince of Humbug.

For most of his early career, Barnum was known as a displayer of oddities. In 1842 he opened the American Museum in New York, and people flocked in to see what was collected there: giants, dwarfs, the Bearded Lady, the Feejee Mermaid (sewn together from a monkey and a fish), and more. Barnum kept crowds moving through with a big sign pointing the way to the "Egress"—the exit. Gullible museumgoers who followed the sign (thinking that Egress was some kind of oddity) found themselves outside. Eventually Barnum took his collection on tour, in the United States and Europe. He went bankrupt in 1855, and when the museum burned down in 1868, he announced his "retirement" from show business.

The star attraction of Barnum's museum and tours was Charles Stratton of Bridgeport, Connecticut—better known as General Tom Thumb. A midget, Tom Thumb sang and danced, and he charmed audiences everywhere. In Britain, he even gained several audiences with Queen Victoria. He had his own coach, barely three feet high and drawn by four small ponies. In time, his share of the money from admission tickets made him very wealthy. But he spent all the money and was poor when he died at the age of 45.

Barnum's "retirement" didn't last long. By 1871 he was back in business, this time with a huge show called "The Great Traveling World's Fair." It included a menagerie, a sideshow, acrobats, tightrope walkers, and clowns. Equestrian acts (*above*) were a big part of the show, which had 200 horses. Aerialists (*left*) were among the leading stars. The show traveled from town to town in a caravan of wagons, and it was a great attraction. Although Barnum changed his business partners and the name of his show several times, he had found his vocation as proprietor of a circus. He first used the title "The Greatest Show on Earth" for his three-ring extravaganza in 1876.

LILLIE TURNOUR
PREMIER TRAPEZIST
OF THE WORLD.

MISS
JESSIE LEON.
DARING EXPONENT OF
THRILLING AERIAL SENSATIONS

MISS
NETTIE CARROLL
PHENOMENAL AERIAL
BICYCLIST & EQUILIBRIST

The great showman didn't always deal in circuses and sideshows. Early in his career, he brought the Swedish singer Jenny Lind to the United States. Her 1850 tour was a great success, and she became one of the best-loved singers of the day. Barnum also had a career in politics. He served in the Connecticut state legislature in the 1860's and as mayor of Bridgeport in the 1870's, and he even once ran for Congress.

Perhaps the crowning moment of Barnum's circus career came in 1882, when he acquired Jumbo from the London Zoo. Jumbo was said to be the largest elephant in the world, and Londoners were furious when they heard he was to leave Britain. The publicity about the purchase was so great that people flocked to see the beast when he arrived in New York. Within weeks, Jumbo had earned ten times his purchase price. He remained a circus star until his death in 1885.

The Barnum & Bailey Greatest Show on Earth

By the time Jumbo joined the circus, Barnum had a new partner: James A. Bailey. Bailey ran a competitive circus, and in 1881 he merged with Barnum. Like Barnum, he was a great showman. The Barnum and Bailey circus traveled as far west as Texas, in a special train sixty or seventy cars long. Posters like those shown here announced the circus. And a brigade of advance cars preceded the train, drawing people with the sound of a steam calliope and stereopticon pictures of the fantastic acts to come. Bailey sold his interest in 1885, but his name remained with the show.

Although the circus played in many cities, it was perhaps best loved in small towns. In an age without television, Barnum's traveling shows brought entertainment to places that otherwise would have had none. For many people—especially children—the arrival of the circus in town was the high point of the year. Those who couldn't pay the price of admission tried to see the show any way they could, peeking under the canvas to catch a glimpse of the strange animals, clowns, and daredevil acts inside.

Barnum died on April 7, 1891. In his will, he left instructions that his show go on—and it has. Now called the Ringling Brothers and Barnum & Bailey show, it's one of the largest, most colorful, and most spectacular circuses in the world. Many of the acts are the same as they were in Barnum's day—fearless aerialists, bareback riders, clowns, and trained animals of all sorts. And when the circus comes to town, it's still an exciting moment. Doubtless, P. T. Barnum would approve.

CLOWNING AROUND

"Clowns are pegs on which to hang a circus," P. T. Barnum once said. And it's true —clowns pull the whole show together and make it run smoothly. They tumble into the arena between acts, and they keep the audience in constant chuckles while other acts are going on. For many people, clowns are the high point of the circus, the best part of all.

What does it take to be a clown? A lot more than a funny suit and some makeup. Modern clown characters developed over the centuries from characters in the pantomime plays that were popular in Europe during the 1500's and 1600's. Today a clown may spend years developing his or her spe-

cial character and appearance. A clown must also have a stock of dozens of gags and be skilled in such arts as juggling, unicycle riding, stilt walking, and acrobatics.

Where do circuses find people with these skills and talents? The Ringling Brothers and Barnum & Bailey Circus, for one, trains them. In 1968 the circus opened Clown College in Venice, Florida. Competition for admission to this college is stiff: Each year 4,000 to 5,000 hopeful clowns apply for training, but only 60 are accepted. Of those, fewer than 20 will be offered performing contracts by the circus after they've finished their training.

The Clown College course lasts about two months, and students work hard. They start the day with morning exercises. Then they attend classes in acrobatics and the other skills they'll need as professionals. They practice their stunts and gags until late at night. Their goal is to be ready for a performance at the end of the course. At that performance, the circus producers will select the new clowns for the show.

Probably the most difficult part of becoming a clown is developing a character. Hopefuls spend hours putting together their costumes. They spend even more hours staring into mirrors, studying their faces and trying out different makeup effects. Developing a character is very important. No two clowns are alike—each is an individual. But there are three traditional types of clowns: the whiteface clown, the auguste (rhymes with *boost*) clown, and the character clown. Students must decide which type they want to become, and then figure out what individual characteristics they'll add to the traditional look.

Whiteface clowns (opposite page, top) are scheming rogues. They're the ones who throw pies, pitch buckets of paint, and generally get the other clowns in trouble. They're descended from Harlequin and Pierrot, characters in early European pantomimes. In the 1600's, pantomime players powdered their faces with flour so that they'd stand out. Today whiteface clowns make up with greasepaint, which is usually made of zinc oxide and olive oil. The greasepaint is spread over the clown's face, neck, and ears. Then the clown adds color—a red

nose (perhaps made of putty), a big red grin, raised black eyebrows, and other details. Whiteface clowns often wear gorgeous costumes of satin and spangles, but some go in for clashing plaids and crazy polka dots.

Auguste clowns (center) are on the receiving end of whiteface clowns' pranks. They're the ones that fall down, get doused with water, and just can't seem to do anything right. (The name "auguste" originated in Germany in the 1800's, where it was a slang term for clumsy or silly.) This clown type is most closely related to the pantomime character Pierrot. An auguste clown wears outlandish clothes that are yards too big, and has a pinkish face highlighted with white patches, a bulbous nose, and a big grin. Wide eyes give the face a continually puzzled look.

Character clowns (bottom) are newer than the other types. The character may be anything—a bumbling policeman, a little old lady, a clumsy ballplayer. One of the most famous characters is the sad-eyed tramp, dressed in tattered tails and battered hat. Tramp clowns are very versatile and often give solo performances. But it's very difficult to develop this character. As one tramp clown put it, "It really needs twenty years' experience to carry the makeup."

The tramp clown usually sports a wide red or white mouth, a red nose, and a gray, unshaven chin. A well-meaning soul, the tramp often tries to do impossible tasks. The famous tramp clown Emmett Kelly, for example, would try to sweep away pools of light cast by spotlights on the arena.

By the time they graduate from Clown College, the new clowns will have been suited up from head to toe. (It costs about $2,000 to outfit a professional clown—those huge, floppy shoes alone can cost $125 or more, and a hand-sewn yak-hair wig in an outrageous color can run $250.) They'll also know how to sew and how to take care of their costumes, since once they're on the road they'll have to do their own washing and mending.

The new clowns will continue to develop their characters and add to their collections of gags as the years go by. And they will get better and better at their job—making you laugh.

GLASS REUNION

"Three years!" Doc said, leaning on his pickax. "My! How flime ties!"

"You mean how time flies," Grumpy snorted.

"That's what I said," Doc replied.

Happy held up his hands. "Shoosh, you two!" he said. "We don't have time to argue. We've got to *think!*"

What the Seven Dwarfs had to think about was an anniversary gift for Snow White and her Prince. Time, as Doc had tried to say, had indeed flown. In just two days, it would

be the royal couple's third wedding anniversary. There would be a big celebration at the castle and everyone would bring an anniversary present. But the Seven Dwarfs still hadn't decided on a gift for the happy pair.

Now, as the Dwarfs went back to work in their diamond mine, each of the little men was lost in thought about what to give Snow White and the Prince. Dopey picked up a large, sparkly diamond from the diamond cart and held it up.

Sneezy translated Dopey's gesture. "Dopey says we can give her diamonds!"

Doc shook his head. "Not this time, Dopey! For third wedding anniversaries, you're supposed to give a gift made of glass."

"Silliest thing I ever heard of," Grumpy grumped. Doc shrugged. "That's the rule," he said, swinging his pickax. Then, as his pickax struck the wall of the mine, something very strange happened: Part of the wall began to crumble!

"Landslide!" Sneezy hollered, starting to push everybody toward the mine entrance.

"No . . . wait!" Doc said. "Look! It's a *tunnel!*" Doc had uncovered a hidden tunnel in the wall of the diamond mine. Holding their lanterns high, the Dwarfs peeked cautiously into the gloomy passageway.

"Looks awful spooky in there," Bashful said.

"I g-guess we ought to explore it," Doc stammered, hoping that somebody would come up with a better suggestion. But nobody did.

So, with Doc leading the way, the seven little men entered the dark, damp tunnel. As the explorers moved forward, their mine lanterns cast long, spidery shadows against the walls.

sense trying it." Grumpy was a brave Dwarf, but he didn't believe in going overboard about it. Whatever was on the other side of the door could stay there, as far as Grumpy was concerned.

Doc put his hand on the doorlatch. As he touched it, the door creaked open!

The flickering light from the seven lanterns revealed a large, dungeon-like chamber, strung with cobwebs. Against one wall, an ancient bookshelf sagged under the

"Keep close together, men!" Doc whispered. "There are other tunnels going off in all directions. It'd be mighty easy to get lost in here!"

The brave band walked for what seemed to be a very long time, until, at last, the tunnel came to an abrupt end at a great wooden door.

"Probably locked," Grumpy said. "No

weight of massive, leather-bound volumes. In the center of the room, a table held a variety of strange jars, filled with colored liquids and powders. Near the table, on the floor, was a shattered goblet. Dust covered everything.

Happy was the first to speak. "What *is* this place?"

But no one answered because no one

knew. Only Snow White's wicked step-mother had ever known about this room. For this was the room far beneath her castle where the evil Queen had kept her books of spells, her secret compounds, and her Magic Mirror!

And there the mirror was, three years later, on the wall where the Queen had left it on her final day.

"Perfect!" Doc exlaimed, when he saw the elegantly carved and bejeweled mirror. "Men, I think we've just found Snow White's anniversary present."

Two days later, the Seven Dwarfs presented Snow White and the Prince with the mirror, all shined up and sparkling like new.

"It's the most beautiful mirror I've ever seen," Snow White exclaimed. And she thanked each of her seven little friends with a kiss on each of their seven little foreheads.

Immediately, she sent for the Royal Carpenter and instructed him to hang the mirror over her dressing table.

That evening, Snow White seated herself at her dressing table and began to comb her hair, gazing at her reflection in her lovely new mirror.

Then she put down the brush and asked herself: "Now, then, where did I put my hairpins?"

She was so busy looking for them that she didn't notice the odd thing that was happening to her mirror. Snow White's reflection had vanished. In its place was a ghostly, masklike face.

And then, in hollow tones, it spoke!

"Snow White, Snow White search no more!
Your pins are in the second drawer!"

Well, you could have knocked Snow White over with a feather! "Who-who said that?" she managed to say.

The mirror answered her question.

"Infinitely wise am I,
  Knowing all of earth and sky.
Or, to put it somewhat clearer,
  'Twas I who spoke—your Magic Mirror."

"My word!" said the Prince when Snow White told him about the Magic Mirror. "I'm sure the Seven Dwarfs don't know about this, or they would have mentioned it when they gave it to us. We must return it to them. It wouldn't be fair for us to keep it."

The next morning Snow White and the Prince put the Magic Mirror in the royal coach and drove to the Dwarfs' diamond mine.

As the coach approached the diamond mine, six of the Seven Dwarfs ran out to meet it. "Thank goodness you've come!" Doc said. "Dopey's lost in the tunnel!" Sneezy added quickly.

"The dern fool went back for his lantern all alone," Grumpy said. "He left it in that place where we found the mirror."

Little by little, Snow White and the Prince made sense out of the story. Dopey had wandered off into one of the many side tunnels that led away from the main passage. Since Dopey couldn't yell for help, they couldn't tell which tunnel he was in.

The Prince said he would go back to his castle at once and return with his soldiers to help look for Dopey.

But Snow White had another idea. "Let's ask the Magic Mirror to help us."

Magic Mirror? The Dwarfs looked at each other in wonder.

The Prince took the mirror out of the coach.

"Please help us find Dopey, Magic Mirror," Snow White pleaded.

Once again, the ghostly face appeared in the glass.

"To find your wandering friend, Snow White,
  Look in the third tunnel on the right!"

Once Dopey had been found, it was unanimously decided that Snow White and the Prince should keep the mirror. And, in appreciation for what the Magic Mirror had done for him, Dopey came over to Snow White's castle every Saturday morning and polished it.

HUNGRY PLANT...POOR ANT

Travelers in space have landed on a strange planet far from Earth. In single file, they walk warily through a jungle of unfamiliar plants with odd, twisted forms. Suddenly one of the party cries out in surprise—the tendrils of a vine have wrapped around his body and are pulling him into the brush! The others rush to help him, shouting in terror, "Man-eating plant!"

Small wonder that the characters in this make-believe scene are surprised and frightened. In nature as we usually think of it, animals eat plants—not the other way around. Plants draw nourishment from the soil and then convert it into energy with the help of sunlight, through a process called photosynthesis. Animals then get nourishment from plants. Horses and cows eat grass, for example, and you enjoy fruits and vegetables.

But did you know that right here on Earth, there are plants that turn the tables on this natural order and actually get most of their nourishment by eating animal life? It's true —but there's no need to be afraid. Most of these plants aren't large enough to devour anything much bigger than a moth. A few of the largest species might manage a small frog or lizard, but even so, insects are their usual dinner.

These carnivorous (meat-eating) plants make up a very small portion of the plant life on Earth. Some of them are very rare. But others are more common—you might even find one in a bog or a swampy area near your home, because marshes are a carnivorous plant's usual habitat.

Scientists aren't sure why these plants have developed the ability to eat insects, but they have a theory. Plants must have certain nutrients, especially nitrogen, to thrive. In the marshy areas where these plants generally grow, the soil is often very poor in nutrients. But nitrogen and other nutrients are contained in the amino acids that form the proteins in animal tissues. Thus these plants may be getting the nutrients they need by trapping and digesting insects.

Of course, catching insects isn't all that easy—if you've ever tried to swat a buzzing fly, you know how difficult it can be. How

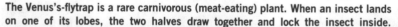

The Venus's-flytrap is a rare carnivorous (meat-eating) plant. When an insect lands on one of its lobes, the two halves draw together and lock the insect inside.

does a plant, which is rooted to the ground, manage to do it? The various carnivorous plants have developed different methods, but the basic idea is the same: they lure the insect in with some sort of attractive bait, and then trap it so that it can't escape.

VENUS'S-FLYTRAP

The plant called Venus's-flytrap is one of the rarest of the carnivorous plants. It grows only in a few marshy spots along the coasts of North and South Carolina. Because these plants are such curiosities, people often want to dig them up and take them home. Now so few are left, conservationists are afraid the plant may die out.

The Venus's-flytrap is a small plant. It bears white flowers on a stalk about 12 inches (30 centimeters) tall. Branching out from the base of the flower stalk are leaves that may be 6 inches (15 centimeters) long. Every leaf ends in a pair of hinged lobes that face each other, like the two halves of a clamshell. (In fact, this shell-like appearance helped give the plant its name—a seashell was the symbol of the ancient Roman goddess Venus.) Each pair of lobes is rimmed with long, sharp spines; the inner surfaces of the lobes have six sensitive hairs, which tell the plant when an insect alights.

The lobes are the plant's fly-catching mechanism. They produce secretions that are very attractive to insects. When a fly or some other insect is lured by the secretions and lands on the lobes, it touches the sensitive hairs. If it touches one hair, nothing happens. But when it touches a second—SNAP! The lobes draw together, and their spines lock the fly inside like prison bars.

Tiny insects may be able to escape through the spines, but they have to do so quickly. In a few minutes the lobes slowly begin to press tighter and tighter together, crushing the insect. Then the plant begins to secrete digestive juices. Digestion may take anywhere from one to ten days. When the plant has finally finished its meal, the lobes open up again, ready for the next victim.

SUNDEWS

Sundews are relatives of the Venus's-flytrap; in fact, they belong to the same plant family, *Droseraceae*. There are 120 kinds of

The sundew's leaves bristle with reddish hairs, each one tipped with a blob of a sticky secretion. When an insect alights on the plant, it's trapped by the gluey fluid.

sundews. There are species on all the continents of the world, although sundews are most common in Australia and in southern Africa. The most common species in North America is the round-leaved sundew. It bears white flowers on stalks about 10 inches (25 centimeters) tall, and it has a cluster of round leaves that are about the size of small coins. (Some species of sundews have leaves

that are teaspoon-shaped; still others have leaves that are 2 feet, or 60 centimeters, long.)

A sundew's leaves bristle with reddish hairs. Each hair is tipped with a blob of a sticky secretion. In the sunlight, these blobs glisten like dewdrops. When an insect is drawn to one of the leaves by the glitter, it is quickly trapped by the gluelike fluid on the hairs. Then the hairs on the edge of the leaf bend in over the unfortunate bug to make sure that it won't escape, and the leaf begins to secrete digestive juices that will break down its body tissues. When digestion is complete, the hairs unbend and begin to secrete more glittering glue.

BUTTERWORTS AND BLADDERWORTS

Butterworts grow in the swampy areas of most northern countries. They are small plants with attractive flowers—the common butterwort, which is found in North America, has violet blooms on tall stems. The plant's leaves lie close to the ground, forming a cluster at the base of the flower stalk.

Like the sundews, butterworts use glue to catch their prey. The leaves arc covered with a sticky secretion that draws insects to them. When the insect lands, the leaf curls up to trap it and digest it.

Although butterworts use the same trapping methods as sundews, they belong to a different plant family—*Lentibulariaceae*, the bladderwort family.

Most bladderworts are aquatic plants— they grow right in water. The common bladderwort, which is native to lakes and bogs in North America and Europe, is sometimes grown in garden ponds. It has spikes of showy yellow flowers that bloom above the water. Below the surface is the rest of the plant—a network of thin roots and stems and small, feathery leaves. Attached to the leaves are many tiny, hollow, balloon-shaped "bladders." The bladders help keep the plant afloat, and they're also the plant's insect traps.

Underwater insects and insect larvae are the bladderwort's prey. The mouth of each bladder is surrounded by sensitive hairs and covered by a trap door that will open only inward. When an insect brushes against the hairs, the walls of the bladder suddenly expand, creating suction that opens the door and pulls the insect inside. Then the door slams shut, and the insect is digested.

PITCHER PLANTS

Several species of pitcher plants grow wild in the swamps and bogs of North America. They range in height from 2 to 3 feet (60 to 90 centimeters) and carry purple or yellow flowers. And pitcher plants have yet another method of trapping their meals.

Shortly after the plant blooms each spring, it sprouts its pitchers—long tube-shaped leaves, sometimes with a flap arching over the opening at the top. The rim of each tube is streaked with color so that it resembles the petals of a flower, and it is baited with a sweet "nectar." When an insect comes to investigate and lands on the edge of the tube, it slips on the slick secretion, falls inside, and is trapped—the inner walls of the tube are covered with stiff hairs that point down, preventing the bug from crawling up and out. Gradually the insect slides deeper and deeper into the pitcher, until it falls into a pool of rainwater and digestive juices at the bottom.

Not all insects fall victim to the plant. One type of mosquito actually lives inside pitcher plants—it hovers about in a helicopter-like fashion without getting trapped in the hairs. A species of fly lays its eggs right in the trap. When the larvae hatch, they secrete enzymes that protect them from the plant's digestive juices, and they help themselves to the plant's dinner. And the larvae of a certain type of moth can actually kill the plant. The moth larva enters the pitcher and spins a web across the opening, cutting off the plant's food supply. Then it begins to eat the plant. Finally it pupates in the withered plant, emerging as an adult moth.

But moths aren't the pitcher plant's greatest enemies—people are. Like the Venus's-flytrap, the pitcher plant has been collected because it is an oddity. And as marshes are drained to build roads and homes, the plant's habitat is being destroyed. In some areas, the plants have nearly died out, and several types are classified as endangered species. Now conservationists are working to protect these strange animal-eating plants that have successfully turned the tables on nature.

A pitcher plant's tube-shaped leaves are baited with a sweet nectar—which lures unsuspecting insects inside.

GREETINGS IN THE ROUND

Would you like to send someone an extra-special greeting card? No card is more special than one you make yourself. Here are some cards that are so pretty, the people you give them to may even want to use them as wall decorations.

These cards require two basic "ingredients"—construction paper and paper doilies. Most doilies are round, but occasionally you can also find heart-shaped doilies. And most are white, but red, gold, and silver doilies are available, too.

Begin by cutting out colorful backgrounds from the construction paper. These should be slightly larger than the doilies. If you use two white doilies—one atop the other—you'll need two backgrounds. These can be the same or contrasting colors.

You don't have to use an entire doily. For example, you can remove a doily's center, as was done for the card above. (Save cutout parts to decorate the envelope.)

Glue together the layers of the card, being careful to center them. Then cut out a circle of white paper and glue it to the back of the card. That's where you will write your greeting. Make the writing circle smaller than the card itself, so that there will be a colorful border.

Now you're ready to decorate the card. Here's where you can really be imaginative. Bows, stickers, sequins, glitter, tiny artificial flowers—these are just a few of the materials you can attach to the card. You may wish to match the decorations to the occasion. For example, use hearts

and flowers if it's a romantic card. Or match the card to the interests of the person you give it to. If the person is into rock music, use a sticker of a favorite group.

You might even try your hand at making a matching envelope for the card. Make it from the same color construction paper you used for the card. Decorate the envelope by gluing a small piece of doily on the front, in the lower left-hand corner.

ANIMAL TAILS

The longest tail ever measured belonged to a dinosaur known as *Diplodocus*. One of the shortest tails belongs to people. In between, tails range from a pig's skinny twirl to a peacock's dazzling train.

A skeleton of *Diplodocus* is on view at the Carnegie Museum of the Natural Sciences in Pittsburgh, Pennsylvania. The dinosaur's neck measures 22 feet (7 meters), its body 15 feet (5 meters), and its tail 50 feet (15 meters). The tail alone is longer than a city bus. *Diplodocus* probably used its gigantic whiplash tail as a bone-crushing weapon against enemies.

Humans have barely a hint of a tail. It's a small bone at the base of the spine, shaped like a cuckoo's beak. It's called the *coccyx* (KOK-siks), from the Greek word for "cuckoo."

Short or long, plain or fancy, tails are important. Some animals can't get along without them. They're used for flying, jumping, running, swimming, sitting, eating, hunting, fighting, keeping warm or cool, warning friends, scaring enemies, and flirting with the opposite sex.

TAILS THAT SEND MESSAGES

When a beaver hears or smells anything suspicious, it smacks the water with its large, paddle-shaped tail. This danger signal sounds like a sharp gunshot. And it warns all the beavers within hearing to quickly race for safety.

The beaver's tail has other uses, too. In the water, it serves as a rudder—a beaver lowers its tail when it dives and raises it when it swims back to the surface. On land, the tail becomes a sturdy prop—when a beaver sits upright to feed or to cut down a tree, it supports itself with its broad, flat tail.

A white-tailed deer sends a silent warning signal with its tail. At the first sign of danger, it flicks its tail upward. The top of the deer's tail is dark, but the underside is pure white—the only white patch on the animal's body. The sight of this white patch flashing in the woods instantly alerts all the deer in the herd.

Some tails are used to scare off enemies. A rattlesnake shakes its tail when it feels threatened. As the rattles at the tip of the tail click together, they make a buzzing sound—

When you see a skunk lift its black-and-white tail like a battle flag . . . watch out!

a warning that the rattler is ready to strike. The rattle isn't a signal to other rattlesnakes, since snakes are almost deaf. A rattler can't even hear its own rattle. Instead, its rattle may save the snake from being stepped on or attacked.

A skunk also depends on its tail to keep enemies at a distance. When you see a skunk lower its head and lift its black-and-white tail like a battle flag, it means that the skunk is getting ready to fire. If you don't retreat fast, the skunk will twist into a U-shaped position, aim both head and tail at its target, and let go with its stinking spray.

Some birds use their tails to send a different kind of message. Male birds often have large, colorful tail feathers that they show off during courtship displays. When a peacock spreads his long tail feathers, or train, he wants to attract the attention of females. He opens his train by shaking himself until the brilliant feathers rise behind him and spread out like a lacy fan. Then he struts about, clattering his quills together, screaming loudly, and turning around slowly as the peahens watch.

The Australian lyre bird gets its name from its big lyre-shaped tail. During his courtship display, a male lyre bird not only shows off his tail, he also sings, dances, and does imitations. As a female watches, he spreads his tail wide, throws the tail over his head, and turns in a half-circle. Then he stands on tiptoe and shakes his tail feathers. He turns again and again, jumping forward and stepping back, snapping his tail closed, then spreading it open again. During this dance, he sings the lyre bird's melodic courtship song and also imitates the songs and calls of many birds and other animals.

TAILS FOR MOVING ABOUT

Without tails, birds would have a hard time flying. In the air, a bird drives itself forward with its wings, but it steers and balances with the help of its tail. When a flying bird turns, it spreads its tail like a fan and twists the tail in one direction or the other to help swing its body around. When it moves upward or downward, it bends its tail up or down. As it lands, it lowers its widely spread tail, which acts as a brake.

Long-tailed birds like swallows can turn sharply at high speeds as they dart about chasing insects. Short-tailed birds like ducks can't steer nearly as well. They never make quick turns while flying. Short-tailed birds are also poor landers, since they find it diffi-

cult to slow down. A duck usually lands on water, pushing its webbed feet forward and skidding to a stop.

Most fish would be helpless without their tails. A fish uses its tail as a propeller. It swims by twisting its body and beating its tail fin from side to side. A fast swimmer like a marlin or swordfish has a large forked tail fin, which it beats back and forth with great force.

A fish's tail fin is upright, or vertical. Whales, dolphins, and porpoises have tails that are flat, or horizontal. They beat their tail flukes up and down, like the flippers on a skin diver's feet, as they dive down into the depths, rise to the surface to breathe, or swim straight ahead.

On solid ground, tails help many animals keep their balance as they run and jump. Fast runners like wolves and cheetahs must constantly twist and turn as they chase their dodging prey. They bend their long tails in the direction they want to turn, just as speeding bicycle riders lean inward while turning to keep their balance.

Powerful jumpers like kangaroos also need their long tails for balance. A kangaroo's outstretched tail balances the weight of its body as it leaps through the air, covering 30 feet (9 meters) with a single bound. Without its tail, the kangaroo would topple over when it tried to jump. Like a beaver, a kangaroo also uses its sturdy tail as a support when it sits upright.

The long tails of many tree-dwelling animals help them maneuver through the treetops. A squirrel uses its bushy tail to keep its balance as it races along branches and runs headfirst down tree trunks. When it leaps to the ground from a high branch, its tail serves as a parachute and a brake. Flying squirrels spread their wide tails like sails as they glide long distances from one tree to the next.

Some tree dwellers have long prehensile (pre-HEN-sul) tails—tails that can grasp a limb or other object and hang on. A prehensile tail is like a long arm with one strong finger at the end, in place of a hand. South American spider monkeys, woolly monkeys, and howlers have such powerful prehensile tails that they can swing from branches, supporting their entire body weight with just the tips of their tails.

A spider monkey can reach out with its tail and grab a piece of fruit hanging at the end of a branch. It can wrap its tail around a

A kangaroo needs its long tail for balance when it jumps. It also uses its sturdy tail as a support when it sits upright.

Even a baby opossum knows what to do with its prehensile tail—grasp a tree limb and hang on!

branch and hang on while it sleeps. If it misses its mark as it leaps from tree to tree, it can check its fall by seizing a branch with the tip of its tail. Even a baby spider monkey uses its prehensile tail, to hang on to its mother.

Another animal with a strong prehensile tail is the opossum, which also hangs upside down from branches. An opossum often uses its tail as a safety belt, anchoring itself to one end of a branch while reaching with its paws for ripe fruit at the other end. When baby opossums are big enough to leave their mother's pouch, they climb onto her back and cling to her fur with their tiny feet and their little prehensile tails as she climbs trees in search of food.

TAILS FOR HUNTING

Alligators and crocodiles often hunt with their tails. A crocodile will lie in wait along a riverbank, waiting for deer or pigs to come and drink. Once an unsuspecting animal gets close enough, the crocodile lashes out with its powerful tail, hurling the victim into the water and then attacking with its toothy jaws.

The thresher shark uses its tail to catch fish. The upper part of its tail fin is longer than the shark's body and is curved like a scythe. Lashing the water with its long, curved tail, the shark herds schools of small fish into a tight bunch, so it can easily gulp them down.

The Willie wagtail is a bird that is native to Australia. When it is hungry, it swishes its long tail feathers through the grass, stirring up insects in the process. As the insects fly up from the ground, the wagtail grabs and eats them.

TAILS FOR SELF DEFENSE

Few animals are foolish enough to attack a porcupine. Buried beneath its long fur, a porcupine has more than 30,000 sharp quills, and lots of those quills are in its tail.

If a porcupine is threatened, it raises its quills, turns it back to the enemy, and lashes out with its tail. A single slap of that bristling tail can drive hundreds of barbed quills into the enemy's flesh. Like fishhooks, the quills catch under the victim's skin. After attacking a porcupine once, most animals learn their lesson. They never try it again.

Another dangerous tail belongs to the African pangolin, or scaly anteater. A pangolin looks like a walking pine cone. It's covered with flat, sharp-edged scales from the top of its head to the end of its long tail. The scales stick out along each side of its tail, like the blades of a double-edged sword. A pangolin's lashing tail can rip into an enemy.

In the sea, stingrays have tails like whips, armed with poisonous spines as sharp as daggers. When a stingray is disturbed, it flicks its tail from side to side or snaps the tail over its head, driving its spines into the enemy. Some stingrays have two or three poisonous spines on their tails. And some of those spines are more than a foot long.

Tails for self defense: A porcupine's tail contains sharp quills that act like fishhooks when slapped against an enemy. A stingray's whiplike tail is armed with poisonous spines that are as sharp as daggers.

The tropical surgeon fish is armed with a pair of small switchblades, one on either side of its tail. Each blade is as sharp as a surgeon's scalpel. Normally the blades are flattened shut against the fish's tail fin. But in an emergency, the surgeon fish can snap open the blades and strike sideways with its tail.

The tail of an electric eel packs a real jolt. In the eel's tail are bundles of special cells that build up electricity. As the eel swims through South American rivers, it gives off a weak electric current. When it finds food or is alarmed, it can deliver a strong electric shock of 650 volts. It uses the electricity in its tail to stun the fish and frogs it feeds on, and to jolt enemies like alligators.

Some tails save the lives of their owners by breaking off if they are grabbed by an enemy. Many lizards have long tails that snap off easily. Often the tail will wriggle violently on the ground after it breaks off, holding the enemy's attention while the lizard escapes. In a short time, the lizard grows a new tail that may save its life again.

MORE TAILS

Cows and horses use their tails as fly swatters. You've probably seen two horses standing side by side, facing in opposite directions, flicking their tails as they shoo flies from each other's faces.

Songbirds sometimes use their tails as umbrellas for their nestlings. During a rainstorm, a robin will spread its wings and tail feathers over its nest, keeping the nest and the chicks dry.

A lizard called the Gila monster is one of several animals that store food in their tails. Gila monsters live in desert regions where food is often scarce. When they have a chance, they eat more than they need. The extra food is changed to fat and stored in the Gila monster's tail for future use, just as a camel stores body fat in its hump.

Tails can also keep their owners warm or cool. Foxes and squirrels wrap their furry tails around their faces while sleeping in winter. In summer, animals like mice, beavers, and muskrats sweat through their nearly naked tails. Without such tails, the body heat in these thick-furred animals would build up to dangerous temperatures.

A lizard called the Gila monster stores fat in its tail, just as a camel is able to store body fat in its hump.

TAILS THAT EXPRESS FEELINGS

A tail can sometimes tell you how an animal feels. Squirrels flick their tails when they're nervous. The more nervous they become, the faster their tails flick.

A frightened mouse vibrates its tail. When a house cat is frightened or angry, its tail swells up to three times its normal size as the tail's fur stands on end.

Members of the dog family express several emotions with their tails. A dog holds its tail high when it feels perky and confident. If it feels playful, it wags its tail slowly, with wide sweeps. If it wants approval, it holds its tail lower, and wags it more quickly. And if it is being scolded, what does it do? It hides its tail between its hind legs.

RUSSELL FREEDMAN
Author, *Tooth and Claw*

CUTTING UP

You probably know Hans Christian Andersen best as the author of *The Ugly Duckling* and *The Emperor's New Clothes*. But did you know that the great Danish storyteller was also something of an artist?

Hans Christian Andersen loved to experience and observe—and these experiences and observations were woven into his fairy tales. Sometimes, however, he would record special memories by making small ink drawings or papercuts. He especially enjoyed creating papercuts. With a pair of scissors, he would cut out his fantasies—a ballerina in a bird's nest, a droll figure balancing a town atop its head, a puppet with doors and windows. Some of his paper cutouts were used as Christmas decorations—such as the fanciful dolls you see on these pages.

Andersen's papercuts can be found in Odense, Denmark, in the house where he was born in 1805. This house has since become the Hans Christian Andersen Museum. There, you can also find letters, portraits, and first editions of his fairy tales. You can even see Andersen's personal belongings, including his hat case, umbrella, walking stick, and the length of rope he always carried in his travels—in the event of a fire at his hotel.

But which of the many tile-roofed buildings in Odense is the museum? Just look for the big gold papercut of the sun over the entranceway!

THE COLD GIANT

Once upon a time there was a cozy little village, nestled in a warm and sunny valley. The folks who lived there were very friendly. They worked hard, played hard, and cared about each other. A boy named Ivan and his family lived there, too.

The people in this village didn't have much, but they shared whatever they could. They didn't have any money, but they didn't need any. Whenever a person wanted something, he would barter, or trade, for it. There were no robbers, no tax collectors, and no parking meters. That's because there were no cars, which was just as well, because there weren't any gas stations, either.

For as long as anyone could remember, there had been a big old castle on the hilltop overlooking the valley. And for as long as anyone could remember, the castle was off limits to everyone in the village.

One day Ivan asked his mother about the castle on the hilltop.

"That's where the cold giant used to live," she told him.

"The cold giant?" asked Ivan. "Doesn't he live there anymore?"

"No, he went away a long time ago," Ivan's mother went on, "but while he was here, this valley was an awful place to live. The sun never shone and the skies were always gray and cloudy. It snowed every day, so children never played outdoors and nobody ever visited their neighbors. Nobody cared much about anyone else."

Ivan wondered what happened to make this such a nice place to live.

"When the cold giant went away," Ivan's mother answered, "the sun came out and melted the snow. Then the children came out to play, and neighbors visited other neighbors. People began to care about one another."

Ivan couldn't imagine not being able to play with his friends outdoors. He was glad the valley was a warm and friendly place to play, but he kept wondering about the cold giant.

"Mother, what did he look like?" Ivan asked.

"Nobody knows," his mother replied. "Nobody ever visited the castle or talked to him. We never even saw him leave, but everyone was glad when he was gone."

When Ivan woke up the next morning, he looked out the window and saw something he had never seen before. There was snow on the ground! It had probably snowed all night, because the snow was waist-deep everywhere.

Everyone in Ivan's family was bundled up in sweaters and robes when Ivan went down to the kitchen for breakfast.

"Is the cold giant back?" Ivan asked his mother.

"I think so." Ivan's mother shivered. "Put another log on the fire and come eat your oatmeal," she said, with a hint of sadness in her voice.

Ivan put a log on the fire and came back to the kitchen, where he and his family ate breakfast in silence.

After breakfast Ivan sat at the window watching the snow fall. He felt sad that he wouldn't be able to go out and play with his friends.

Many days went by. Ivan was getting tired of staying indoors, and he wondered what his friends were doing. He was also tired of just wondering about the cold giant in his castle on the hilltop. So he decided that after everyone had gone to sleep, he would go up to the castle and see for himself.

That night, after a dinner eaten in silence, Ivan's family all went to bed early. There really wasn't anything else to do.

After he was sure that everyone else was sound asleep, Ivan got out of bed and dressed in his warmest clothes. Then, taking a lantern in his hand, he set out for the cold giant's castle.

The warm glow from the lantern's flame cast eerie shadows on the shimmering snow as Ivan trudged cautiously up the hill toward the cold giant's castle.

When he got there, Ivan found the front door to the castle open, allowing the snow to swirl into the hallway. Ivan held the lantern as high as he could and stepped carefully through the door. The frost-coated floor crunched beneath his feet as he walked into the castle.

At the end of the hallway there was an enormous room, and at one end of the room there was a fireplace that hadn't been used for a very long time. A huge staircase led to the second floor, where a door opened into the cold giant's bedroom.

Peeking nervously around the door, Ivan saw a great big bed covered with several great big blankets. There, shivering under the blankets, his teeth chattering, lay the cold giant.

Suddenly, Ivan had an idea. He hurried back home and very carefully and quietly grabbed two logs from the woodpile. With one log tucked under each arm and some kindling in his pocket, he quickly retraced his steps to the cold giant's castle.

A spider had made its home in the huge unused fireplace, and Ivan was careful to shoo it away before he laid the fire. He lit the kindling from the flame in his lantern.

As he nursed the flames to life, Ivan began to feel sleepy. After all, it was way past his bedtime. So he curled up at one end of the huge couch in front of the fireplace. By the time the fire was blazing merrily, Ivan was sound asleep.

Soon the warmth from the fire reached the cold giant's bedroom. The giant stopped shivering and his teeth stopped chattering. Throwing off his blankets, the cold giant shuffled out of his bedroom and downstairs. "Who dares to come into my castle and light a fire in my fireplace?" the cold giant wondered to himself.

But when the giant saw the fire crackling and popping cheerfully in the fireplace, he

stopped wondering about who had started it. He plopped himself down in front of it and wiggled his toes. He started to feel warm and cozy for the first time in a long time. As he began to thaw out, the flickering flames made shadows that danced on the walls. The cold giant giggled at the images.

The giant's giggles awakened Ivan. He watched the giant wiggle and giggle and began to think of him as just another one of his friends—someone he could play with. So it was only natural that Ivan giggled, too.

"Who's there?" roared the giant, leaping to his feet. He spotted little Ivan curled up on the couch. He leaned down and stared at the boy.

"Who are you to laugh at me?" he demanded. "Who said you could come here? I don't need heat! I don't need company! I don't need—"

But it was too late. Ivan already knew what the giant was really like. He had heard how he giggled. He had seen his toes wiggle. So Ivan wasn't afraid of him. Before the

"That's nice, dear," his mother said. "Why don't you bring him home to meet us?"

"Gee, Mom, that's a great idea," said Ivan. "He's just the nicest fellow. I gave him a hug, and he gave me a hug, and we're going to have hot cider when I get back to the castle."

"Ivan, wait a min—" his mother began, but Ivan quickly grabbed another armful of logs, and went running back up the hill.

Everybody in the village thought that the cold giant had gone away again and taken the cold weather with him. When Ivan came down the hill with his new friend the giant, everyone was surprised. How could the giant still be here, when the valley was warm and friendly?

"All it took was a few logs," explained Ivan.

Ivan's mother understood. She knew that the logs had very little to do with it.

"All it really took was one little boy who wasn't afraid to reach out and hug," she said with pride.

And from that sunny morning, they all lived happily and warmly ever after.

giant could say anymore, Ivan reached up, put his arms around the giant's neck and gave him a great big hug.

Before the cold giant knew it, he was hugging the little boy back. His giant arms lifted Ivan off the couch, and tears trickled down his giant cheeks. He hadn't been hugged in so long that he'd forgotten how good it felt.

The giant set Ivan down with a smile. "Now, sit by the fire with me," he said. "We will have some hot cider."

"Oh, that would be fun," Ivan replied. "But first I have to do something. I'll be right back." And the boy scampered out of the castle and back down the hill.

Ivan was halfway home before he realized that it had stopped snowing. The sky was clear and the flowers had begun to bloom. All the children in the village were playing outdoors, and neighbors were once again visiting over backyard fences. Warmth had returned to the valley.

"Mother! Mother!" Ivan called as he burst through the front door. "I have a new friend!"

MARK TWAIN
REMEMBERED

He probably wouldn't have liked all the "fussin'." He didn't care much for ballyhoo, and he loved to poke fun at grandness. One of his pet peeves—and he had many—was the observance of anniversaries. "What ought to be done to the man who invented the celebrating of anniversaries?" he wrote in his notebooks. "Mere killing would be too light."

Whether he would have liked it or not, American author Mark Twain was celebrated for *three* anniversaries during 1985: the 150th anniversary of his birth, the 75th anniversary of his death, and the 100th anniversary of the publication of his masterpiece, *The Adventures of Huckleberry Finn.* From Calaveras County, California, to the banks of the Mississippi, to Hartford, Connecticut, America marked the occasion with a year-long series of special events—parades, stage productions, museum exhibits, lectures, and readings of his works.

Mark Twain loved nothing more than spinning yarns. In addition to *Huckleberry Finn,* he wrote *The Adventures of Tom Sawyer* (1876), *The Prince and the Pauper* (1882), *A Connecticut Yankee in King Arthur's Court* (1889), several other novels, a handful of travel and adventure books, and more than a dozen collections of stories, essays, and sketches. As a lecturer, he delighted audiences with humorous accounts of his youth, his travels, and the people he met. And in his parlor room, he entertained guests for hours with jokes, anecdotes, and tall tales.

The trademark of Twain's stories was their simple, colloquial style. Using the direct, home-spun language of ordinary folk, Twain displayed a keen sensitivity to people, their hopes, and their pretenses. He was more than a humorist—he used his stories to attack meanness, false pride, and foolishness. In slangy, conversational tones, he conveyed the ordinary virtues of humility, decency, and common sense. Although Mark Twain was popular in his own time, his reputation has grown enormously since his death. His stories and characters have become part of America's national folklore.

A BOY AND A RIVER

Mark Twain was born Samuel Langhorne Clemens on November 30, 1835, in the village of Florida, Missouri. When Sam was 4, his parents moved the family to nearby Hannibal, on the banks of the Mississippi River. Growing up in Hannibal, Sam became enchanted with the life and lore of the great river. The Mississippi was a lifelong fascination, and it provided the material for many of his greatest books. Sam later took the name Mark Twain as a reminder of life on the Mississippi—when riverboat crews charted the depth of the river, they would cry "mark twain!" to indicate a measure of 2 fathoms (12 feet).

Young Sam left school at the age of 11 to become a printer's apprentice. He worked in Hannibal for a newspaper published by his brother, Orion, and then found jobs in St. Louis, New York, and Philadelphia. After a year in Iowa, again working for Orion, Sam was drawn back to the Mississippi. In 1857, traveling down the river, he persuaded the steamboat captain to teach him how to pilot. After earning his license, he served as a river pilot until the Civil War, when the Mississippi was closed to commercial traffic.

ADVENTURER AND TRAVEL WRITER

After serving with the Confederate Army for two weeks, Clemens quit and set out for the western frontier in 1861. For the next several years, he lived with Orion in the Nevada Territory, trying his hand at gold mining, the lumber business, and other unsuccessful ventures. On the strength of humorous sketches he had been writing about his adventures in the West, Sam landed a job with a newspaper in Virginia City, Nevada. He began signing his articles "Mark Twain."

Twain moved on to San Francisco in 1864, joining the staff of *The Morning Call* and writing for two local magazines. In 1865 a New York magazine published his short story about a California frog-jumping contest, called "The Celebrated Jumping Frog of Calaveras County." The story made him famous overnight. During the next several years, Twain began lecturing and continued his writing as a travel correspondent for several publications. In 1867 he sailed on the *Quaker City* to Europe and the Middle East, sending back comic but insightful letters about his experiences. The letters were later made into a book, *The Innocents Abroad* (1869), which won him worldwide attention and financial freedom.

NOVELIST, LECTURER, FAMILY MAN

In 1870, Twain married Olivia Langdon, the sister of a fellow traveler on the *Quaker City*. Olivia was from upstate New York, where the couple lived briefly after their marriage. In 1871 they moved to Twain's favorite city, Hartford, Connecticut. The house they built there was a Victorian-style mansion, with an ornate design that suggested a Mississippi River steamboat. It was to be their home for twenty years.

Huck Finn (*right*) and Tom Sawyer look for adventure in this statue at Hannibal, Missouri. An inscription at the bottom reads: "A Tribute to Mark Twain."

HUCKLEBERRY FINN AT 100

We catched fish and talked, and we took a swim now and then to keep off sleepiness. It was kind of solemn, drifting down the big, still river, laying on our backs looking up at the stars, and we didn't even feel like talking loud, and it warn't that often we laughed—only a little kind of low chuckle. We had mighty good weather as a general thing. . . . Other places do seem so cramped and smothery, but a raft don't. You feel mighty free and easy and comfortable on a raft.

The story is about a homeless 14-year-old named Huckleberry Finn. Fleeing his father, Huck meets up with a runaway black slave named Jim. Together Huck and Jim escape down the Mississippi River on a raft, drifting by night and hiding out by day. Huck is an irresponsible but good-hearted boy without much schooling, and he tells the story in his own words. Life on the river is free and peaceful. Along its shores, however, Huck and Jim meet up with thieves, swindlers, murderers, and lynch mobs. Much of the book's appeal lies in the loyalty between Huck and Jim as they help each other through adventure and mishap. The boy learns from Jim about the worth and dignity of a human being.

In 1985, the 100th anniversary of its publication, *The Adventures of Huckleberry Finn* continued to delight readers of all ages. First published in the United States in 1885, the book sold more than 50,000 copies in its first three months. Since then some 20,000,000 copies have been bought in the United States and other countries. Huck Finn has been translated into 30 foreign languages, and it has been made into a movie six different times. To mark the anniversary, a Broadway musical called *Big River* opened in spring, 1985. Also, several publishers put out commemorative editions of the book, one of them selling for $1,500. Huck would have had a pretty big belly laugh over that price!

Once dismissed as "vicious trash" and "cheap, pernicious stuff," *Huckleberry Finn* is now regarded as Mark Twain's masterpiece and a classic of American literature. Literary critic Lionel Trilling called *Huck* an "almost perfect work." And Ernest Hemingway, the great 20th-century author, once said: "All modern American literature comes from one book by Mark Twain called *Huckleberry Finn*. There was nothing before it. There has been nothing as good since."

Nevertheless, the book remains a source of controversy. Critics say it is racist in its treatment of the black slave Jim. Contending that the book has no place in the classroom, some schools and libraries have even banned it from their reading lists and bookshelves. But defenders of Twain say that the book actually is an attack *against* slavery and racism.

At the age of 100, Huck Finn was still making trouble!

One hundred years after its publication, *The Adventures of Huckleberry Finn* was put to music. And *Big River* (below), the rousing stage show based on the Mark Twain masterpiece, was one of Broadway's biggest 1985 hits.

The Hartford years were the most creative in Twain's writing career. There and in Elmira, New York, where the family spent summers, he produced many of his most important works. *Tom Sawyer, Life on the Mississippi* (1883), *Huckleberry Finn, A Connecticut Yankee,* and other books made him one of the best-known and most prosperous authors of his time. Twain also went on long lecture tours, packing auditoriums across the United States and Europe. And when he wasn't working, he enjoyed spending time with his three daughters—Susy, Clara, and Jean. As young girls, Twain's daughters loved to act out his stories, especially *The Prince and the Pauper.*

Despite his great success, Mark Twain suffered deep disappointments during his later years. He lost his entire fortune in two unsuccessful business investments—a publishing firm and a new kind of typesetting machine. That forced him to move his family to Europe, where they could live more cheaply. Then, while he was away lecturing, his daughter Suzy died of meningitis. Twain's outlook darkened, and his writing became gloomy and pessimistic. His wife's health also began to fail, and she died in 1904. Jean, his youngest daughter, died five years later.

In the last months of his life, Mark Twain recalled that he had been born when Halley's comet was shooting across the night sky. "It will be the greatest disappointment of my life if I don't go out with Halley's comet," he said. The day after he saw Halley's return, on April 21, 1910, Twain died at his home in Redding, Connecticut. And, as if it had been planned, the special events marking the Twain anniversaries of 1985 were capped by the year-end re-appearance of Halley's comet.

JEFFREY H. HACKER
Author, *Carl Sandburg*

FOR ENDANGERED SPECIES ONLY

Elephants, tigers, bears—these are the kinds of animals you expect to see at the zoo. But on the island of Jersey, in the English Channel, there's a special kind of zoo that has none of the usual beasts. The residents of the Jersey Zoo are all members of endangered species—rare animals that are threatened with extinction.

The zoo was founded in 1959 by British naturalist Gerald Durrell, who began his career by collecting animals for regular zoos. He soon realized that many of the animals died in captivity. And he became concerned about the rare species that were in danger of dying out entirely. His answer was to set up his own zoo. The zoo is financed by a non-profit group, the Jersey Wildlife Preservation Trust, which is active in conservation projects around the world. Its symbol is the dodo, a flightless bird from the island of Mauritius in the Indian Ocean. The dodo became extinct in the 1600's, largely through human carelessness.

What do the thousands of people who visit the Jersey Zoo each year see? There are lowland gorillas, several kinds of lemurs, snow leopards, and orangutans from Sumatra. There are also African crested porcupines; spiny tenrecs from Madagascar and the Comoros Islands; and rare monkeys, such as the golden lion tamarin from Brazil.

There are rare snakes, lizards, and tortoises in the reptile center, including some Mexican box terrapins. A number of reptile species (gecko, skink, and boa) come from Round Island, in the Indian Ocean. About 100 years ago, people introduced goats and rabbits to that island. The animals ate most of the vegetation, and as a result the reptiles began to die out.

The zoo has more than 40 rare species of birds from around the world, including white-winged wood ducks, bare-faced ibis, St. Lucia parrots, pink pigeons, and white-eared pheasants. A special house is home to a group of Rodrigues fruit bats. When thirteen of these bats arrived at the zoo in 1978, they represented ten percent of the world-wide population.

Whenever possible, the zoo tries to make its animals feel at home by putting them in natural surroundings. For example, the wallaby enclosure has eucalyptus trees and birds from Australia. And the gorilla area is a natural landscape with a stream, boulders, and trees for the apes to climb. It's surrounded by a deep moat, so that you can see the gorillas without peering through cages.

The residents of the Jersey Zoo are animals that are threatened with extinction—such as this spiny tenrec . . .

The animals are well cared for. They are examined by veterinarians once a week. And each species has a special diet, carefully designed to be as close to the natural diet as possible. To provide the animals with the food they need, the zoo has its own vegetable and fruit farm.

But the Jersey Zoo's goal is not simply to put these rare animals on display. The hope is that in their natural surroundings, the animals will feel comfortable enough to breed. Then, rather than declining, the numbers of these endangered species will increase, and they can be re-introduced to their native lands.

The zoo has had a great deal of success with its breeding programs. Eight lowland gorillas have been raised, and they're now being studied to see how gorilla family groups interact. And many species of birds have been bred. Pink pigeons have been raised at the zoo and then returned to their native land, Mauritius. More than 100 rare Rothschild's mynas from Bali, and over 200 white-eared pheasants, have been hatched at the zoo and sent to various places around the world. Bats and reptiles and even snails have been successfully bred.

The Jersey Zoo also provides researchers with an opportunity to study rare animals that they might otherwise not find in nature. In addition, it runs a training program for zookeepers and conservation workers. Students come from all over the world. They work in each of the zoo's sections, learning how to care for different types of animals. And they learn how to breed wild animals in captivity. It is hoped that when they return home, they will use these methods to save their own countries' wildlife.

Not all the conservation work takes place at the zoo. The Wildlife Preservation Trust International, a sister organization with headquarters in Philadelphia, supports similar programs around the world. For example, the group helped develop a captive breeding program for golden lion tamarins in Brazil, and it's helping to set up a similar program for black-footed ferrets in Wyoming.

Not more than 88 of the ferrets remain. But with luck, the wildlife conservationists will be able to save these and other endangered animals from extinction.

. . . and these golden lion tamarins.

FASCINATING DESERT DWELLERS

You can travel to many parts of the world and see cacti. In southern Europe, rows of prickly pear cacti are used to mark property boundaries. In Sicily, cacti are cultivated as a source of food. In Egypt, India, and Australia, there are cacti growing in the wild. But these fascinating plants are native only to the Americas. Those found elsewhere were brought there by people or perhaps grew from seeds carried over the ocean by birds.

SPECIALLY ADAPTED PLANTS

In the Americas, cacti can be found from southern Canada to the tip of South America. The greatest variety, however, are found in the deserts of northern Mexico and the southwestern United States. There, you can see a spectacular array of cacti, including the giant of the desert—the saguaro. This plant, which may live. for hundreds of years, reaches heights of more than 40 feet (12 meters). It is one of the largest of all cacti. At the other end of the size scale are such species as the living rock cacti, which may be only 2 inches (5 centimeters) in diameter.

There are some 1,500 species of cacti. All are members of the family *Cactaceae*. "Cactus" comes from *kaktos,* the ancient Greek word for thistle.

Cacti are plants that have especially adapted to the harsh, dry conditions of the desert. And that is why cacti look so different from other green, flowering plants: They are usually leafless with spine-covered stems and branches.

A few members of the cactus family have leaves that are similar to more familiar plants. The pereskia, which grows in the West Indies and Central America, is one example. But the leaves of most cacti have developed into spines or hairs, which protect the plant from hungry animals. The spines and hairs grow from small cushionlike structures on the stems and branches. These structures are called areoles, and they are arranged in patterns over the surface of the

Most of the 1,500 species of cacti have flamboyant flowers. Clockwise, from top left: pincushion cactus; hedgehog cactus; prickly pear cactus; barrel cactus; giant saguaro cactus.

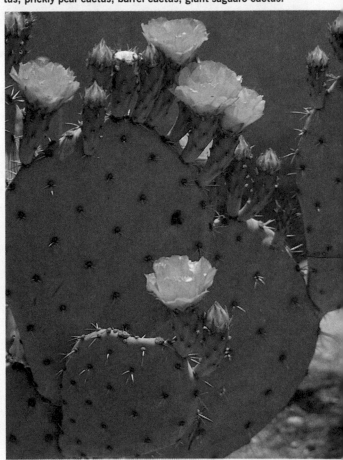

plant. Branches and flowers also grow from the areoles. Even cacti with leaves have areoles. Areoles are a botanical characteristic that all cacti—and no other plants—share.

In most other plants, the leaves make the food and, in the process, give off water to the air. But since most cacti have no leaves, the stem of the plant has taken over the job of making food. And the stem gives off very little water. In fact, it serves as an excellent storage tank.

A cactus stem contains large amounts of spongy tissue designed to hold water. When

A gilded flicker uses the giant saguaro for nesting. When the flicker leaves, other birds will take up residence.

it rains, the plant's large root system rapidly absorbs water from the soil. The water travels up into the spongy tissue, swelling the cells. Huge amounts of water may be taken in. A giant saguaro can absorb more than 200 gallons (757 liters) of water during a single storm.

Not only does the stem store water, it also has a waxy coating that slows water evaporation from the plant. Even the spines and hairs that cover the stem may help restrict evaporation by filtering the strong sunlight—in much the same way Venetian blinds filter light coming through a window.

Another distinguishing feature of cacti is their large, often flamboyant flowers, which are usually shaped like funnels or wheels. The flowers vary in color from white to red, purple, and orange. They have many petals and sepals (modified leaves), which are often identical in shape and color. Some cactus flowers are long lived. The tiny peanut cactus, for example, produces bright red flowers that last several weeks. Other cacti have flowers that live only briefly. The flowers of the queen-of-the-night cactus bloom for only one night. These fragrant flowers may be a foot (30 centimeters) long and 8 inches (20 centimeters) wide.

After the cactus flower dies, a berrylike fruit forms. It is filled with many seeds. A giant saguaro fruit contains about 2,000 seeds. And a mature saguaro produces 100 or more fruits each year. That's 200,000 seeds annually! Why, then, aren't the deserts covered with saguaros?

Some of the fruits are gathered by people, who use them for food. The Papago Indians of the American Southwest have long used saguaro fruits to make jam and wine. Many fruits and seeds are eaten by insects, birds, and rodents. Others land in areas that aren't suitable for germination. Among those saguaro seeds that do germinate, less than one percent of the seedlings live for a year.

Growth among the survivors is slow. It takes fifteen years for a saguaro to reach a height of 1 foot (30 centimeters), and more than 40 years for it to reach 10 feet (3 meters). The plant won't grow branches until it is 75 years old. And after it has become a giant, it can fall victim to one of its main enemies—people.

A PRICKLY SUBJECT

Many cacti are destroyed as desert lands are turned into housing developments. Others are wiped out by road building and strip mining operations. "Cactus rustling" has become a serious problem in the American Southwest, and the saguaro is probably the species most often stolen. Rustlers dig up the cacti and sell them to plant collectors and landscapers. Often, however, the roots are damaged in the process, and the plants die.

Some southwestern states have strict laws against the removal of cacti. Violators are subject to fines and imprisonment. In Arizona, legally harvested and imported cacti must be marked with special tags. Owners are expected to keep these tags to identify their plants. If "cactus cops" find untagged plants in people's gardens, they remove the plants and transfer them to public land.

There are good reasons for such tough measures. Cacti roots hold the desert's thin layer of topsoil in place. Without them, wind and water would quickly erode the soil. In addition, many birds and other animals depend on cacti for nesting and food. Mourning doves and wrens, for example, make their nests in the bristling cholla cactus. The plant's sharp spines don't bother these birds, but they keep away the birds' enemies. Gila woodpeckers and gilded flickers drill nest holes in the giant saguaro. After they raise their young, they abandon the nests. But the nests rarely stay vacant for long. Martins, crested flycatchers, screech owls, and other birds soon take up residence.

One of the advantages of a home inside a large cactus is a built-in cooling system. On a hot summer day, the temperature in one of these nests may be 30°F (16°C) lower than that outside.

Once cacti are removed from the desert, they are hard to replace because they grow so very slowly. It has been pointed out that it takes 70 years for a rainbow cactus to grow as tall as this book . . . and less than a minute for a cactus rustler to dig it up.

If you want to grow your own cacti, you should purchase plants grown in nurseries. Or you can grow plants from seed or from cuttings. In this way, you can help ensure the survival of some of nature's most fascinating and beautiful plants.

GROW YOUR OWN CACTI

Cacti are easy to grow. They adapt well to the dry, warm environment found in most homes, and they can go for days or even weeks without care. For happy, healthy plants, here are some guidelines for you to follow:

Light. Cacti need lots of light. If little natural light is available, place the plants under overhead lighting fixtures. If light comes from only one direction, turn the plants occasionally so all sides are equally exposed to the light.

Temperature. Cacti will do best in homes where daytime temperatures are about 70°F (21°C) and nighttime temperatures are above 50°F (10°C).

Air. Cacti should be placed in a location that is well-ventilated but not drafty.

Soil. A layer of gravel should be placed in the bottom of the container, to improve drainage. Then add a mixture of one part soil or potting mix, one part leaf mold, and two parts sand.

Water. Like all plants, cacti need water, But too much water will quickly kill these plants. During the growing season, from spring through autumn, give the plants enough water so that the soil is moist but not soggy. During winter, the resting season, water sparingly; let the soil dry completely before watering.

Fertilizer. Fertilize sparingly, if at all, during spring or summer. Bonemeal or a weak solution of 10-10-10 fertilizer is best. Never fertilize during the resting season.

INDEX

ILLUSTRATION CREDITS
AND ACKNOWLEDGMENTS

15 Courtesy Heath Co.
16 Courtesy Androbot, Inc.;
   Courtesy TOMY
   Corporation; Courtesy
   RB Robot Corporation
17 Courtesy OWI Inc.;
   Courtesy Axlon Co.
18–Reproduced by
19 permission of Green Tiger
   Press, La Jolla,
   California, from the book
   Hanimals, conceived by
   Mario Mariotti, with
   color photographs by
   Roberto Marchiori. ©
   1980 by La Nouva Italia
   Editrice S.P.A. Florence,
   Italy
21–Artist, Susan M. Waitt
23
25 © Carleton Ray—Photo
   Researchers, Inc.; John J.
   Smith
26 © R. Carr—Bruce
   Coleman, Inc.; © William
   Harlowe—Photo
   Researchers, Inc.; © E.
   R. Degginger—Earth
   Scenes
27 © V. P. Weinland—
   Photo Researchers, Inc.;
   © Jerome Wexler—Photo
   Researchers, Inc.; ©
   Robert Lee—Photo
   Researchers, Inc.
28 © Patti Murray—Earth
   Scenes; © Gail Rubin—
   Photo Researchers, Inc.
29 © David Overcash—
   Bruce Coleman, Inc.; ©
   Zig Leszczynski—Earth
   Scenes
30–© Jacques Lamontagne
31
32–Courtesy Scholastic
35 Photography Awards,
   conducted by Scholastic
   Magazines, Inc. and
   sponsored by Eastman
   Kodak Company
41 © Leah Painter Roberts
42 Jenny Tesar

43 Solution: "Love Me,
   Love My Cat"; Artist,
   Michèle McLean
45–© Gary Sinick
48
49 © Maurice Fraley
50–© Peter D. Capen—Terra
51 Mar Productions
54–Reprinted from *Owl*
55 magazine with permission
   of the Young Naturalist
   Foundation
56–Jenny Tesar
57
58 © Tracey Frankel
59 © Tracey Frankel; ©
   1984 Budd Symes
61 Steve Powell—*Sports
   Illustrated*
66–Artist, Michèle McLean
71
72 © Michael Fogden—
   Animals Animals
73 © Zig Leszczynski—
   Animals Animals; ©
   Michael Fogden
74 © Zig Leszczynski—
   Animals Animals; ©
   Michael Fogden—
   Animals Animals
75 © Michael Fogden—
   Animals Animals; © Zig
   Leszczynski—Animals
   Animals
76 © Jane DiMenna
80–Artist, Susan M. Waitt
81
82 © Ronald Cohn—The
   Gorilla Foundation
83 © D. M. Rumbaugh
84 The Mansell Collection
85 © Guildhall Library; The
   Bettmann Archive
86 Mary Evans Picture
   Library; The Bettmann
   Archive
87 Mary Evans Picture
   Library; The Mansell
   Collection
88 Circus World Museum
89 The Bettmann Archive;

© J. Messerschmidt—Bruce
Coleman, Inc.
91 © Randa Bishop
96 © Howard Miller—Photo
   Researchers, Inc.
97 © Ken W. Davis—Tom
   Stack and Associates
98 © James R. Fisher—
   Photo Researchers, Inc.;
   © Breck P. Kent—Earth
   Scenes
99 © John Shaw—Bruce
   Coleman, Inc.; © Joe
   McDonald—Bruce
   Coleman, Inc.
100–Crafts by Jenny Tesar
101
102 © E. R. Degginger—
   Bruce Coleman, Inc.
104 © Tom McHugh—Photo
   Researchers, Inc.
105 © Leonard Lee Rue III—
   Animals Animals
106 © Anthony Bannister—
   Animals Animals; © Mike
   Neumann—Photo
   Researchers, Inc.
107 © Zig Leszczynski—
   Animals Animals
108–H. C. Andersens Hus,
109 Odense, Denmark
114 The Bettmann Archive
115 © Ted Schuetz—
   Spectrum Photo
116 Martha Swope Associates
118–© Robert Rattner, 1984
119
120 © John Gerlach—Tom
   Stack and Associates
121 © Robert C. Simpson—
   Tom Stack and
   Associates; © Bob
   McKeever—Tom Stack
   and Associates; © John
   Gerlach—Tom Stack and
   Associates; © Tom
   McHugh—Photo
   Researchers, Inc.; ©
   Richard Jepperson—
   Photo Researchers, Inc.
122 © C. Allan Morgan—
   Peter Arnold, Inc.